AUTHORITATIVE GUIDE TO

Betting Thoroughbreds

The Blood-Horse

AUTHORITATIVE GUIDE TO

Betting Thoroughbreds

BY THE STAFF AND CORRESPONDENTS
OF BLOOD-HORSE PUBLICATIONS

Lexington, Kentucky

ECLIPSE
PRESS

Library of Congress Control Number: 2004113197

ISBN 1-58150-119-6

Printed in China
First Edition: May 2005

Distributed to the trade by
National Book Network
4720-A Boston Way, Lanham, MD 20706
1.800.462.6420

A Division of
Blood-Horse Publications
Publishers Since 1916

COVER PHOTOGRAPH BY MATT GOINS

Contents

Introduction

Perhaps you are attending the races for the first time. Or maybe you attend only a couple of times a year but still want success at the betting windows. Or maybe you enjoy a day at the races but find betting intimidating.

You're not alone. Most people who spend an afternoon at the track are just like you. They are there to have fun with friends and family, watch beautiful Thoroughbreds compete, and hopefully cash a ticket or two — if they can figure out how to place a bet or even pick a possible winner.

The Blood-Horse Authoritative Guide to Betting helps you figure out the often-confusing process of handicapping a race and placing a bet.

In Part I — Betting Basics, we take you step-by-step through an example of the past performances you will find in a racetrack program or in the *Daily Racing Form*, and explain just what all those perplexing abbreviations and numbers mean. You will also learn how racetrack odds are determined and the possible payoffs you'll receive; how essential the information on the tote board is; and what exactly all those poles around the track signify. Most important is the chapter on types of wagers, which details each wager — from a straight win bet to an exacta box to a pick six — as well as how to calculate the cost of each bet and what to say to the mutuel clerk when you place your bet.

As you gain confidence as a bettor, you may want to expand your betting ability by learning more about handicapping a race. But where do you start? In Part II — Handicapping Factors, we delve further into this intricate art. You will learn some of the many factors that go into handicapping a

ANNE M. EBERHARDT

Anyone can learn to bet with a little help.

7

race. For instance, you will find out how important a horse's post position is, as well as what medications can be given to horses on race day and why you should take these factors into consideration when handicapping. Equipment changes, morning workouts, jockey overweights, and track condition are also explored. The section also offers overviews of speed figures, pedigree handicapping, and trip handicapping, explaining what they are and how they can help you make more informed betting decisions. A handicapping analysis of a race pulls all of this together, giving you an idea of how to apply the various handicapping factors when you're at the racetrack.

The Blood-Horse Authoritative Guide to Betting includes a glossary, resource guide, and frequently asked questions, plus "myth busters," a section that addresses certain common misconceptions about betting at the track.

Keep this easy-to-use guide handy when you go to the track and use it to help make your day there more enjoyable and, hopefully, more successful.

PART I

Betting Basics

How to Read Past Performances

Some people bet names. Or maybe they like gray horses. Some wager on the prettiest silks. But to real handicappers, the answer lies within the past performances.

For those who pursue handicapping as if in pursuit of the Holy Grail, the past performances are essential. Sure, countless other factors besides those contained within past performances affect a handicapper's thinking. If a track has been favoring horses with speed or runners that race nearest the rail, only dedicated horseplayers will ascertain those tidbits of knowledge. Studying training patterns can inform horseplayers which trainer has been doing especially well with his three-year-olds but not with his two-year-olds. But the information about each horse contained in its past performance lines is necessary to every handicapper as he or she begins the process of evaluating a race.

As the very name implies, "past" refers to the previous races run by a horse while "performances" means that the collective information in a single line explains how a horse performed in that particular race.

Does a horse perform better when breaking from an inside post position? That can be determined by examining the past performances.

Does a horse do well when switching from turf to dirt races? Check the past performances.

Does a horse run better when the opening quarter-mile of a race is run in :22 or :23 rather than :24 or :25? That information is in the past performances.

A handicapper compares the past performances of every runner in the field to form an image of how the race will be run. That mental picture is then combined with factors the handicapper considers important, such as track bias, pedigree, trainer statistics, and so on.

While past performances won't reveal every potentially relevant piece of information — for example, that a horse was scratched from a similar race five days earlier and the winner of that race won by twelve lengths — the past performance lines do contain dozens of pieces of vital information to help you make a more educated bet.

The following paragraphs examine those parts of the "running"

TRACK PROGRAMS

Large racetrack programs offer tons of helpful hints for handicapping and betting. You can find the following:

- Tips on how to bet and a payoffs chart.
- Professional analysis of the day's races.
- Guide to the past performances.
- Betting terminology.
- Jockey, owner, and trainer standings.
- Profiles of major stakes horses.
- Latest workouts at the track.

SMARTY JONES

Owner: Someday Farr

17

7

18

18

ch.c.4 Elusive Quality–I'll Get Along by Smile
Bred in Pennsylvania by Someday Farm

Trainer: John Servis

05Jun04 Bel11 ft 03 Stk1000000 1 1/2m :48^{65} 1:35^{44} 2:27^{50} -- 9/9 3^1 3$^{1\,1/4}$ 1$^{1/2}$ 1$^{3\,1/2}$ 1$^{1\,1/2}$ 2^1 Elliot
Belmont S. (G 1)
15May04Pim 2 ft C3 Stk1.00000 1 3 16m:47^{32} 1:11^{53} 1:55^{59}**102**6/ 0 1   2$^{1\,1/2}$ 2$^{2\,1/2}$ 2^1 1^5 1$^{11\,1/}$ Elio
Preakness S. G1)

2

1 **5** **6** **3** **4** **16** **8** **9**

How to Read Past Performances

Study this chart of Smarty Jones' Belmont Stakes running line to familiarize yourself with the format.

1	Date of race, race number, track	**11**	Weight
2	Track Condition	**12**	Equipment
3	Distance of Race	**13**	Odds
4	Fractional times	**14**	First three finishers
5	Restrictions	**15**	Comment
6	Type or name of race	**16**	Field size
7	Post position	**17**	Color, age, and pedigree
8	Running position and margin	**18**	Owner, Breeder, Trainer
9	Jockey	**19**	Career Record
10	Medication		

line. Our example is Smarty Jones' Belmont Stakes running line from past performances provided by Equibase Co.:

1. Date of the race, race number, and track: *5Jun04 Bel11* — Indicates the horse ran on June 5, 2004, in the 11th race at Belmont Park. A handicapper will look at how many days elapsed between each race and whether the horse has had long layoffs. Generally, lower level horses, those running say for claiming prices, will run

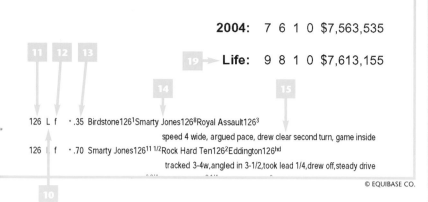

2004: 7 6 1 0 $7,563,535

Life: 9 8 1 0 $7,613,155

126 L f · .35 Birdstone126¹Smarty Jones126⁸Royal Assault126³

speed 4 wide, argued pace, drew clear second turn, game inside

126 l f · .70 Smarty Jones126¹¹ ¹/²Rock Hard Ten126²Eddington126ʰᵈ

tracked 3-4w,angled in 3-1/2,took lead 1/4,drew off,steady drive

more often than those running in stakes races.

Each track has an abbreviation (see table, page 14), and these track "codes" are listed in racing programs and the *Daily Racing Form*, the sport's only daily newspaper containing past performances for tracks around the country. It is important for a handicapper to know at what tracks a horse is racing because purse levels — the amount of money horses run for — vary greatly from track to track. Higher purses generally attract higher quality horses.

2. Track condition: *ft* — This simple abbreviation tells what the condition of the track was for the race. For instance, "ft" or "fst" means fast. If it said "sy" or "sly" that would mean sloppy. Turf races have their own notations. For example, "yl" means yielding and "fm" is firm. While "gd" is good for both dirt and turf courses.

3. Distance of the race: *1½* — For races up to a mile, the distance is shown in furlongs. A furlong is an eighth of a mile. Thus, "6" means the race was six furlongs or six-eighths (three-quarters) of a mile. For a longer race, such as this exam-

ple, the distance is shown in miles. This race was one and a half. If the distance is followed by a symbol consisting of a "T" in a circle, it indicates the race was run on turf.

4. Fractional times and final time of the race: $:48^{65}\ 1:11^{44}\ 2:27^{50}$ — An electronic timing system records the fractional or "split" times of each race, as well as the final time. These are not necessarily the times run by the horse in whose past performance they are contained. Rather they are the times run by the horse in the lead at various stages of the race. Note that Equibase past performances list times to hundredths of a second, while *Daily Racing Form* uses the traditional fifth of a second. In the *Form*, the time(s) of the horse in the lead were :48⅗ for a half-mile, 1:11⅘ for six furlongs, and 2:27⅗ for the one and a half miles.

5. Restrictions: Certain races are restricted by age or sex. The letter "F" inside a circle means the race is restricted to fillies and mares. The number "3" with an up arrow beside it means the race is restricted to horses three years old and older. It is important to a handicapper to know when females race

TRACK ABBREVIATIONS FOR NORTH AMERICAN TRACKS

TRACK	ABBR.	TRACK	ABBR.
Albuquerque, NM	Alb	Kentucky Downs, KY	KD
Aqueduct, NY	Aqu	Kin Park, BC	Kin
Arapahoe Park, CO	ArP	Laurel Park, MD	Lrl
Arlington Park, IL	AP	Lincoln, NE	Lnn
Assiniboia Downs, MB	AsD	Lone Star Park, TX	LS
Atlantic City, NJ	Atl	Los Alamitos, CA	LA
Atokad Downs, NE	Ato	Louisiana Downs, LA	LaD
Bay Meadows, CA	BM	Marquis Downs, SK	MD
Bay Meadows Fair, CA	Bmf	Meadowlands, NJ	Med
Belmont Park, NY	Bel	Monmouth Park, NJ	Mth
Beulah, OH	Beu	Mountaineer Park, WV	Mnr
Calder Racecourse, FL	Crc	Northlands Park, AB	NP
Canterbury Downs, MN	Cby	Oaklawn Park, AR	OP
Charles Town, WV	CT	Ocala Training Center, FL	OTC
Churchill Downs, KY	CD	Penn National, PA	Pen
Colonial Downs, VA	Cnl	Philadelphia Park, PA	Pha
Columbus, NE	Cls	Pimlico, MD	Pim
Del Mar, CA	Dmr	Pleasanton, CA	Pln
Delaware Park, DE	Del	Portland Meadows, OR	PM
Delta Downs, LA	DeD	Prairie Meadows, IA	PrM
Ellis Park, KY	ElP	Remington Park, OK	RP
Emerald Downs, WA	EmD	Retama Park, TX	Ret
Evangeline Downs, LA	EvD	River Downs, OH	RD
Fair Grounds, LA	FG	Ruidoso Downs, NM	Rui
Fair Meadows Tulsa, OK	FMT	Sacramento, CA	Sac
Fairmount Park, IL	FP	Sam Houston Race Park, TX	Hou
Fairplex Park, CA	Fpx	Santa Anita, CA	SA
Ferndale, CA	Fer	Santa Rosa, CA	SR
Finger Lakes, NY	FL	Saratoga Racecourse, NY	Sar
Flagstaff, AZ	FS	Solano, CA	Sol
Fonner Park, NE	Fon	Stampede Park, AB	Stp
Fort Erie, ON	FE	Stockton, CA	Stk
Fresno, CA	Fno	Suffolk Downs, MA	Suf
Golden Gate Fields, CA	GG	SunRay Park, NM	SrP
Grants Pass, OR	GrP	Sunland Park, NM	Sun
Great Lakes Downs, MI	GLD	Tampa Bay Downs, FL	Tam
Gulfstream Park, FL	GP	Thistledown, OH	Tdn
Hastings Park, BC	Hst	Timonium, MD	Tim
Hawthorne Racecourse, IL	Haw	Turf Paradise, AZ	TuP
Hollywood Park, CA	Hol	Turfway Park, KY	TP
Hoosier Park, IN	Hoo	Woodbine, ON	WO
Horsemen's Park, NE	Hpo	Woodlands, KS	Wds
Kamloops, BC	Kam	Yavapai Downs, AZ	Yav
Keeneland, KY	Kee		

against males and when younger horses race against their elders.

6. Type or name of race: *Belmont S. (G1)* — The type of race is always indicated, easily letting the handicapper know what class of race the runner was contesting. Here are the types of races:

Mdn (maiden) — As the name implies, no runner in the race has ever won a race. They are all maidens regardless of how many previous starts they have made.

Alw (allowance) — This means there is some allowance condition that each of the runners fits. For example, non-winners of two races lifetime means none of the horses have ever won two races — at any level — during their careers.

Clm (claiming) — Every horse in this race may be claimed, or purchased, from the race for a desig-

TRACK CONDITIONS

DIRT TRACKS

fst or ft	Fast
wf	Wet-Fast
gd	Good
sly or sy	Sloppy
my	Muddy
sl	Slow
hy	Heavy
fr	Frozen

TURF COURSES & STEEPLECHASES

hd	Hard
fm	Firm
gd	Good
yl	Yielding
sf	Soft
hy	Heavy
gs	Good to Soft (foreign races)
gf	Good to Firm (foreign races)

nated price. The claiming price will also be noted in the past performances. For instance, Clm15000 means the horses could be claimed for $15,000.

Str (starter) — Also called starter allowances, these races have a condition for starting. For example, the race may say limited to horses that have "started" for a claiming price of $10,000 or less.

Stakes — The highest caliber of races are stakes races. They are indicated by the name of the race. In this case, the race was the Belmont Stakes. The most important stakes races are graded stakes and carry either a grade I (G1, the top grade), grade II (G2, the second highest grade), or grade III (G3, the third highest grade). Non-graded races show the name of the race and purse value; graded races show the name of the race and grade.

7. Post position: *9* — This indicates what post the horse broke from in the starting gate. Post one is closest to the inside rail.

8. Running position and margin: 3^1, $3^{11/4}$, $1^{1/2}$, $1^{31/2}$, $1^{11/2}$, 2^1 — At the points during the race where the split times are taken, a person charting the race, called the "chart caller," identifies what place each runner is in and how many lengths he is in front or behind the winner. In this example, the runner at the first call was in third, one length behind; by the time he reached the third "point of call" he had moved into first position, a half length ahead of the second-place horse; at the next call he still had the lead and was three and a half lengths in front; when the field reached the fifth call, he was still on the lead, but only by a length and a half; and at the finish, he was second, one length behind the winner.

A handicapper can compare the runner's placement at each point of call to the split time at each position and see if there is a correlation. Comparing this race scenario to those of past races helps the handicapper get a clearer picture of subtle changes from previous outings. Perhaps a horse won when close to the pace when the fractions of the race were slow. But in his last start, the field went a sec-

POST TIME 3:28.........EXACTA and TRIFECTA Wagers on this Race...Leg A · PICK 3 ...Leg D · PICK 6

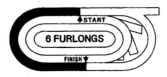

↑START

6 FURLONGS

FINISH ▼

The 19th Running of
THE TRUE NORTH
GRADE II
$100,000 Added
(Up to $17,400 NYSBFOA)

6th RACE   SIX FURLONGS

A Handicap For Three Year Olds And Upward . By subscription of $100 each, which should accompany the nomination; $500 to pass the entry box, $500 to start, with $100,000 added. The added money and all fees to be divided 60% to the winner, 20% to second, 11% to third, 6% to fourth and 3% to fifth. Trophies will be presented to the winning owner, trainer and jockey. Closed Saturday, May 24 with 23 Nominations.

Track Record: Groovy (4), 123 lbs; 1:07-4 (06-21-87)

MAKE SELECTIONS BY NUMBER

M-Line	Owner	Trainer	Jockey
1	Mohammed al Maktoum	W.I. Mott	Pat
	Maroon, White Sleeves, Maroon Cap, White Star		Day
3-1	**Elusive Quality (L)** 115		
	B.c.4,Gone West-Touch of Greatness by Hero's Honor		(4-1-0-1)
2	Lazy Lane Farms	F.L. Brothers	Jerry D.
	Yellow and Lime Green Blocks, Yellow Cap		Bailey
7-2	**Frisco View (L)** 116		
	Ch.c.4,Mt. Livermore-Heaven's Nook by Great Above		(68-19-9-8)
3	Mitchell S. Zimmerman	R. Barbara	Chris
	Yellow and Purple Vertical Halves, Yellow and Purple Halved Sleeves, Yellow Cap		Antley
12-1	**Jamies First Punch (L)** 113		
	B.g.4,Fit to Fight-Stedes Wonder by Native Royalty		(100-15-13-15)
4	Michael Anchel	F. LaBoccetta	Clovis
	Royal Blue, White Braces, Two White Hoops on Sleeves, Blue Cap, White Visor		Crane
20-1	**Raja's Charter (NY) (L)** 112		
	Dk.B./Br.h.6,Raja's Revenge-Jet Setress by Air Forbes Won		(26-1-0-2)
5	Viola Sommer	F. Martin	Julio
	Green, Gold Diamond Hoop, Gold Sleeves, Green Cap, Gold Tassel		Pezua
20-1	**Cold Execution (L)** 112		
	B.h.6,Eskimo-Ax by Ex by Executioner		(45-4-6-4)
6	Kaufman, Iselin and Double R Stable	R. Stoklosa	Jorge F.
	Red and Purple Diagonal Quarters, Red Sleeves, Yellow Chevrons, Purple Cap, Red Visor		Chavez
20-1	**Double Screen (NY) (L)** 109		
	Dk.B./Br.g.4,Double Negative-Video Talc by Talc		(101-15-10-8)
7	William F. Coyro, Jr.	G.C. Contessa	Richard
	Dark Blue, Red Sash, Two Red Hoops on Sleeves, Red Cap, Blue Visor		Migliore
15-1	**Get My Glitter (L)** 110		
	B.g.5,Glitterman-Exuberant Jane by Exuberant		(98-18-8-12)
8	Althea R. Richards	W. Turner	Robbie
	Kelly Green, White Cross Sashes, White Sleeves, Green Dots, White Cap		Davis
9-5	**Punch Line (L)** 122		
	Gr.g.7,Two Punch-Hilarious Astro by Fast Hilarious		(96-12-9-10)
9	Wachtel, Port	H.M. Tesher	John R.
	Gold, Brown Panel, Two Brown Hoops on Sleeves, Gold and Brown Cap		Velazquez
6-1	**Stalwart Member (NY) (L)** 115		
	Ch.g.4,Claramount-Ms. Stalwart by Stalwart		(109-15-18-14)

*(NYSBFOA) New York State Breeding Fund owners award. (Non Purse Monies)
(L) Treated with Lasix; (L1) First time using Lasix; (O) Coming off Lasix

MORNING LINE SELECTIONS 8-1-2

Example of a small track program. Small programs don't contain past performances, so another source, such as *Daily Racing Form*, is necessary to make educated bets.

ond faster at each call and he was lagging behind. The handicapper can make important assumptions from this information.

9. Jockey: *Elliott S* — The name of the jockey is listed, making it easy for a handicapper to see if the rider has been on the horse before. In this case, the horse was ridden by Stewart Elliott.

10. Medication: A capital "B" indicates the horse raced after being treated with phenylbutazolidin, which is a non-steroidal anti-inflammatory. A capital "L" means the horse raced after being treated with the anti-bleeding medication Lasix (now actually called Salix but still indicated by the traditional "L"). (See Chapter 8.)

11. Weight: *126* — This is the weight the horse carried in the race. A handicapper can see what weight the horse has carried in its previous races to see if the horse is adding or dropping weight and if it has previously carried the present weight assignment.

12. Equipment: A lowercase "b" indicates the horse raced while wearing blinkers, which surround the horse's eyes and keep him looking forward. A lowercase "f" means the horse raced while wearing front bandages or wraps.

13. Odds: *.35* — This indicates the wagering odds on the horse in its previous races. For instance, 2.30 means the horse was a bit more than 2-1; his exact odds were $2.30-1. An asterisk before the odds means the horse was the

---

RACE COMMENTS

What exactly do those comments in the past performance lines mean?

- **Altered course:** when a horse changes paths, usually in the stretch run.
- **Blocked/Boxed:** when a horse is caught in traffic and has no running room.
- **Bore in/Bore out:** when a horse sharply veers in or out.
- **Checked:** when a rider has to pull on the reins, altering the horse's stride.
- **Clipped heels:** usually in close quarters; when a horse steps on the heels of another horse causing its rider to take up sharply.
- **Driving:** applies to the winner; a horse that wins under constant urging.
- **Eased:** a horse that is far behind with no chance; rider lets him gallop home.
- **Evenly:** a horse maintains relatively the same position throughout the race.
- **Flattened out:** when a horse moves into a striking position but does not go on.
- **Greenly:** usually applies to horses with little/no racing experience; horse may weave in the stretch or race forwardly, drop back, then come on again.
- **Handily:** applies to the winner; a horse that wins well in command.
- **Hung:** a horse that bids for the lead in stretch but runs out of gas and **flattens out**.
- **Loomed boldly:** when a horse makes strong bid for the lead.
- **Pressed pace:** when a horse with good speed forces the pace set by rivals.
- **Rank:** when a horse fights its jockey and is unmanageable, especially on the lead.
- **Rated:** when a horse relaxes and settles off the pace but in good position.
- **Saved ground:** when a horse races along the rail, taking the shortest path.
- **Speed:** used in conjunction with position on the track to show the horse was prominent to a certain point in the race.

wagering favorite. Thus, *.35 means the horse was favored, and his odds were 35 cents to a dollar.

14. First three finishers, weights, and margins: *Birdstone 126[1], Smarty Jones 126[8], and Royal Assault 126[3]* — These are the first three finishers of the race, the weight each carried, and the margin each was in front of the next finisher. In this case, the 2004 Belmont Stakes, Birdstone won by a length over Smarty Jones, who in turn was eight lengths ahead of Royal Assault, who beat the fourth-place finisher by three lengths. Each of the horses carried 126 pounds. Seeing whom a horse raced against and knowing the weights the first three finishers carried are important pieces of information for the handicapper, especially if the same horses meet again.

15. Comment: *"speed 4 wide,*

argued pace, drew clear second turn, game inside" — The chart caller gives a very brief comment to describe each horse's effort in the race. Often, if a horse had trouble in the race, it is noted here. If the horse won and his race its particularly impressive, that would be noted there. The comment is the briefest of snapshots of the horse's race.

16. Field size: *9* — Field size notes the number of horses in the race. Is this important? If a horse had post position five, it matters if it was a six-horse field or twelve-horse field. Note that in *Daily Racing Form* past performances, the field size is generally listed after the race comment.

17. Color, age, and pedigree: The horse's color and age are given, as is the pedigree — sire—dam, by damsire. Because some sires are more known for the speed they pass on and others are known for things such as siring runners with an affinity for turf, it is important to know the horse's sire (father), dam (mother), and damsire or broodmare sire (father of the mother). The *Daily Racing Form* past performances also list the horse's foaling month after the color, sex, age. The foaling month is

The PPs show which jockeys have ridden a horse during its career.

Race Number

9

Start ↓
6 Furlongs
← Finish

Purse $60,000 Added

Overnight Stakes. **FOR FILLIES AND MARES, THREE-YEAR-OLDS AND UPWARD.** Nominations close on Friday, August 10, 2001 with no fee. $250 to pass the entry box and an additional $250 to start with $60,000 Added, of which all monies to be divided, 60% to the owner of the winner, 20% to second, 11% to third, 6% to fourth and 3% to fifth. WEIGHTS: Three-Year-Olds, 120 lbs.; Older 123 lbs. Non-Winners of $40,000 in 2001 allowed 2 lbs.; $30,000 since October 1, 2000 or $25,000 twice since May 1,2001 allowed, 4 lbs.; (Maiden, Claiming and Starter races not considered.) Two horses having common ties through ownership cannot start to the exclusion of a single ownership interest. Closed August 10, 2001 with 17 nominations. **Six Furlongs**

Track Record: Taylor's Special (5), 118 lbs; 1:08 (08-22-86)   Meet Record: Robin de Nest (4), 117 lbs; 1:09.29 (08-05-01)

Example of a larger track program, which contains at least partial past performances. The information is provided by Equibase Co. and is similar in format to *Daily Racing Form's* past performances.

© EQUIBASE CO.

Probable Favorites 2-5-6

---

important because it only makes sense a horse foaled in January may have a maturity advantage over a horse foaled in June of the same year.

18. Owner, breeder, trainer: The owner, breeder, and trainer of each horse are given, as is the state or country in which the horse was bred. Statistics are also provided for trainers.

19. Career record: These figures give a horse's lifetime number of starts, firsts, seconds, and thirds, as well as career earnings. This information is also usually provided for the current year, past year, off track, dirt, and turf. In this way handicappers can see if the horse has run before on the surface it is running on in is current race, and what its past record has been.

Many, many pieces of information are contained in past performances. Together, they paint a picture of each horse. But as they say about art, "Beauty is in the eye of the beholder." Show the same past performances to a room full of handicappers, and they will not all choose the same horse. That is what handicapping is all about — opinions. It is the opinions of the bettors that determine the odds.

But it all starts with the past performances.

By Dan Liebman

Points of Call

A swimmer in a 200-meter race knows that every time he touches the wall, he is 50 meters closer to the finish. Similarly, when a runner in a 1,600-meter race passes the finish line for the first time, he knows there are three more laps to go. And, should he lose track (no pun intended) with one lap to go, a bell is rung to remind him.

But how does a jockey know how far it is to the finish? Does he glance from the backstretch to the finish line and guess how many feet he still has to travel?

Of course not.

Inside the dirt and turf courses at every racetrack are huge painted poles that serve two major purposes: to house the timing system that keeps track of the fractional and final times of the races and to let the riders know how far it is to the finish line.

The poles are also helpful in other ways; for instance, they help exercise riders work horses at the distance specified by the trainer, and they make it easy for racing fans to keep track of the horses as they progress through a race.

While other sports are measured by meters, yards, and points, racing distances are gauged in furlongs; and racing times, in minutes and hundredths of seconds.

A furlong is an eighth of a mile, and the poles logically are known as the eighth pole, the quarter pole, the half-mile pole, etc. Not a day goes by that you don't hear a fan, or a horseman, say something like, "Did you see the move he made at the half-mile pole?" or, "He didn't give up the lead until inside the sixteenth (half-furlong) pole."

Right away, you have a mental picture of what is being said.

POLE CONFUSION

Knowing which pole is which can be confusing for anyone who watches the races or reads race recaps. Where is the quarter-pole? Or the half-mile pole? How did the chart caller know a horse made a key move at the three-sixteenths pole? The key to understanding the poles is to start at the finish line and work backwards or clockwise around the racetrack.

At North American tracks, the poles are posted at intervals of one-sixteenth of a mile. And they are color-coded:

- Black-striped poles: one-sixteenth-mile markers
- Green-striped poles: one-eighth-mile markers
- Red-striped poles: quarter-mile markers

Working backwards, the first pole is black, or the one-sixteenth pole. The next one is green (the one-eighth or furlong pole); then comes the first red or one-quarter pole. Continue moving clockwise around the track adding a sixteenth for every pole until you reach the finish again. Because track circumferences vary, the number of poles may differ. Just remember to count the poles clockwise from the finish and you'll be better able to understand the race action.

Points of Call

Distance	1st call	2nd	3rd	4th
3½ f	start	1/4	—	str
4f	start	1/4	—	str
4½ f	start	1/4	—	str
5 f	start	3/16	3/8	str
5½ f	start	1/4	3/8	str
6 f	start	1/4	1/2	str
6½ f	start	1/4	1/2	str
7 f	start	1/4	1/2	str
7½ f	start	1/4	1/2	str
1 mile	1/4	1/2	3/4	str
1 m70 yds	1/4	1/2	3/4	str
1 1/16	1/4	1/2	3/4	str
1⅛	1/4	1/2	3/4	str
1 3/16	1/4	1/2	3/4	str
1 1/4	1/4	1/2	mile	str
1⅜	1/4	1/2	mile	str
1½	1/4	1/2	1 1/4	str
1⅝	1/4	1/2	1⅜	str
1 3/4	1/2	mile	1½	str
1⅞	1/2	mile	1⅝	str
2 miles	1/2	mile	1 3/4	str
2⅛	1/2	mile	1 3/4	str

The points of call and fractional times at various distances.

The poles count back from the finish line. Thus, the sixteenth pole is that distance from the finish, not that distance after the start. Knowing the last pole from the finish is a sixteenth of a mile (or a half-furlong) out makes it easy to figure out a horse scored by many lengths when you hear someone say, "He won by a pole."

These easily noticeable poles also have another big function — they mark the points of call that are used in past performances.

Each race comprises a single line within a horse's past performances. As the name implies, "past" refers to the horse's previous races, and "performances" refers to how it performed during those races. Each past performance line gives a number that shows a horse's position (first, second, tenth) at various points during a race. These "points of call" correspond to the poles at which these "calls" of the race are made. The usual points of call, depending on race length, are the start, first quarter-mile, half-mile, stretch, and finish.

ractional Times

5th		Fractional Times		
finish	—	1/4	3/8	finish
finish	—	1/4	3/8	finish
finish	—	1/4	1/2	finish
finish	—	1/4	1/2	finish
finish	1/4	1/2	5/8	finish
finish	1/4	1/2	5/8	finish
finish	1/4	1/2	3/4	finish
finish	1/4	1/2	3/4	finish
finish	1/4	1/2	3/4	finish
finish	1/4	1/2	3/4	finish
finish	1/4	1/2	3/4	finish
finish	1/4	1/2	3/4	finish
finish	1/2	3/4	mile	finish
finish	1/2	3/4	mile	finish
finish	1/2	3/4	mile	finish
finish	1/2	3/4	mile	finish
finish	1/2	3/4	$1^1/_4$	finish
finish	1/2	mile	$1^1/_4$	finish
finish	1/2	$1^1/_4$	1½	finish
finish	1/2	$1^1/_4$	1½	finish
finish	1/2	1½	$1^3/_4$	finish
finish	1/2	1½	$1^3/_4$	finish

When the horses reach a pole that corresponds to one of these points, a chart caller — a person employed to help compile the past performances information for Equibase, the industry's data provider — quickly calls out each name as the competitors pass the pole and how many lengths in front or behind the nearest horse it is at that point.

This information is later put into a computer and becomes a part of each horse's past performance. When a handicapper examines past performances, he easily can see at each point of call how far in front or behind each runner was. Comparing this to the interval times of the races helps the handicapper gauge if the pace of the race influenced the positioning of the horses.

If a horse runs his best when on the lead but is noted at the first point of call as being sixth, twelve lengths behind the leader, this is relayed into the past performance and becomes important information for the handicapper. The

Horses pass a green-striped eighth pole.

handicapper can assume this is why the horse lost the race.

As stated earlier, the points of call vary, depending on the length of the race, though every race from five furlongs to seventeen furlongs has five points of call. The three shortest races, run at three and a half, four, and four and a half furlongs, are the exceptions, each with only four points of call.

Two points of call are the same for every race: the stretch call (an eighth of a mile from the wire) and the finish. As the horses cross the finish line the final time is recorded as are the margins between each horse, from the winner to the last-place finisher. While every race must have a winner — a few, called dead heats, have more than one — every race must also have losers. Where they are when they hit the finish is the most important "point of call" because it defines how many lengths behind, what their approximate time for the race was, and most importantly to horsemen, how much purse money they earn for the effort.

That last point of call is important because it may indicate that a particularly fast, or slow, time was run. Also it is important to know if the winner won by a half-length or ten lengths.

But is the race necessarily better if the winner won in a slow time by five lengths or in a fast time by less than a length? In fact, more information is needed, and that information is gathered as the field passes the other points of call and becomes the past performances.

Want to learn how to read past performances better and become a handicapper? The next time you are at the racetrack, take a look at the poles. Then study the points of call on the race chart or in a horse's past performance lines.

Understanding how the poles and points of calls are connected is an important part of handicapping.

By Dan Liebman

The Tote Board

In an airport, the television monitors provide much of the vital information necessary to help you navigate your way: flight number, concourse, gate, time of departure, status of flight, etc.

At a racetrack, the tote board provides a similar function.

In fact, without the information on the tote board — and hundreds of TV monitors that are microcosms of it scattered throughout the grounds — making an informed wager would be impossible.

The tote board is the lifeblood of the racetrack, as important to the grandstand as the grooms are to the backside barn area. Racehorses couldn't exist without the dedicated grooms who baby them, and racetracks couldn't exist without the bettors who put their $2 wagers through the windows. But those bettors could not make a single wager without the tote board.

Tucked away in the bowels of every racetrack are computers that rapidly input the wagers as they are made and output the odds on every runner in every race, as well as the many exotic, or multiple wagers, now offered.

The process is really quite simple, using a mathematical formula to break the money wagered into pools. Each type of wager has its

Bettors gather before an indoor tote board.

own separate pool. For example, all the dollars bet to win comprise the win pool; to place, the place pool; the daily double, the daily double pool; etc. A computer program figures out the total dollars in the pool and how much has been wagered on each entrant; it then assigns odds to the horses, letting the bettor know how much he will win should the horse he wagers on win the race. The horse with the most money bet on it is the favorite and has the lowest odds.

The computer can make the various calculations so quickly, that in addition to the odds to win, place, and show, it also can figure and display all the possible payouts on every other wager. These payouts, often called "will pays," may be shown on the tote board, but more likely on the televisions.

In fact, the computer can figure wagers made at different tracks or on different days. For instance, several years ago Churchill Downs instituted a wager called the Kentucky Oaks/Kentucky Derby daily double. The wager is made on Friday, Oaks Day, and completed the next, Derby Day.

A programmable mathematical formula determines all odds because the betting line must do what is called "balance." That is, the odds must always be in sync. You can't have a field of ten with four equal favorites, every entrant with odds of less than 8-1, or a field of all longshots.

There are many important pieces of information on the tote board, but clearly the most important is the **odds** of the horses. The odds change every few seconds as racing fans make their wagers, so it's important to check the tote board regularly for updated figures.

Odds are always shown as compared to a $1 bet, with a few exceptions. Seeing 5, 8, or 17 next to the program number of the horse you wish to wager on means the odds are 5-1, 8-1, and 17-1. There are exceptions for horses with odds below even money (1-1) and those from even money to 5-1.

Odds below even money return less than a dollar for every dollar wagered, so they must reflect that on the tote board. For example, 3-5 means you receive $3 for every $5 wagered, or 60 cents for each dollar.

Odds between even money and 5-1 are shown at every 50-cent interval; thus, you might see 7-2, which means $7 returned for every $2 wager. These odds are essentially 3 1/2-1 and give the bettor a more accurate picture of lower-priced odds.

Very high-priced odds are shown at increments of five, thus 60-1, 65-1, 70-1, etc. A

Tote boards provide split and final times.

ANNE M. EBERHARDT

Odds and other key information can be gleaned from the tote board.

horse might actually be 62-1 but would show as 60-1.

The tote provides numerous other bits of key information:

Split and final times of races: An integral part of handicapping is assessing the pace and speed at which you believe a race will be run. On the tote board, the fractional and final times of races are shown. It is important to remember that the fractional times being shown are not of the favorite or the race's eventual winner but of the horse leading the race at the moment each fractional time is recorded.

The fractional, or "split" times as they are called, vary according to the length of race. For a six-furlong race, for example, the quarter-mile (first two furlongs) and half-mile times are the only splits shown, in addition, of course, to the final time. For longer races, more frac-

tional times will be displayed.

The times may be shown in either fifths or hundredths of a second, depending on the track's timing equipment. In fact, some tracks show the times in both. Until a few years ago all times were shown in fifths, and it was common to hear someone say: "He went a tick over a minute," meaning one minute and one-fifth. For years, sports such as swimming, in which several competitors may touch the wall within the blink of an eye, have been using more sophisticated timing systems than horse racing. Now, with such systems not only so advanced but so easy to install and use, it has made sense for racing to switch to a more accurate measure of the abilities of its athletes.

Determining which horses in the field will be on the lead, which ones will be mid-pack in stalking positions, and which ones will be

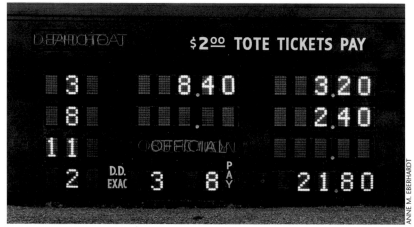

ANNE M. EBERHARDT

Once results are declared "official," payoffs will be posted.

charging from off the pace can be a challenge for handicappers. To do this, handicappers try to estimate the pace of the race, thus explaining a common phrase in racing, "pace makes the race."

With pace so important, many race watchers are anxious to see the fractional times flash on the tote board. A field of horses that runs a second faster or two seconds slower than the handicapper anticipated might explain why the running positions of the horses were not what he predicted.

Program numbers: Sometimes it's hard to find the position of the horse you bet during a race. Tracks have tried to make this easier, by assigning the same color saddlecloth to each horse with the same program number. For example, in every race, the #1 horse would get the red cloth, the #2 horse, the blue, and so on. But another way is watching the tote board, where the program numbers of the four horses in the lead during the race are posted.

An official with the racetrack watches the race through binoculars and calls out the numbers as the horses change positions. With a quick glance at the tote board, you can easily see if your horse is among the first four in the race.

Payoffs: When the horses cross the finish line, there is only one important thing to those holding winning tickets — the amount of the payoff. This will be displayed on the tote board.

First, the order of finish is put up for the first four horses to cross the finish line. In racing, the term "in the money" refers to the first three finishers; the term "hit the board" means the first four because that is how many are displayed on the tote board.

When the race is declared "official," the payoffs for win, place, and show are posted on the tote board. When a longshot wins, there often is a collective gasp when the prices are first posted. Everyone gets a charge out of seeing prices for a winner such as $88.60, $38.80, and $16.40.

Prices for multiple or exotic wagers may also be shown on the tote board, usually in a section below the payoffs for win, place, and show, or to the side.

Inquiries and Objections: When the numbers of the first four finishers are displayed on the tote board but before the race is official, you may notice the program number of one or more horses blinking. In this case, an inquiry or objection is taking place.

Sometimes during the running of a race, a horse impedes or bothers another horse. A group of three judges, called stewards, watches each race through binoculars and on television monitors to see if an infraction has occurred. If they see what they believe might be a cause for a disqualification, the inquiry sign is illuminated on the tote board. If a jockey in the race feels he has been fouled, he informs the stewards before the race is official and the objection light is turned on.

In either case the stewards review the race from different vantage points on television replays. They can look at a "pan" shot or side view, while also having access to head-on and rear views of the race. They can watch the race in slow motion and judge whether the claim necessitates a disqualification. Stewards make a judgment call in determining if the incident altered the outcome of the race.

Official: Never discard a tote ticket until the race has been declared "official." A sign on the tote board will be illuminated just before the payoffs are posted.

Photo Finish; Dead Heat: When the photo finish sign is lighted, it means a finish is so close, a photo is being developed to determine who finished in what position. When the dead-heat sign lights up, it means two horses have tied for a finish position.

Time of Day; Minutes to Post: This may seem obvious, but it is surprising how many times during a racing day you find yourself needing to know how many minutes remain until post time. Losing track of time is easy, and the tote board is the easiest place to see the current time and the number of minutes until post time for the next race.

Overweights; Changes: Under the "conditions" of a race, jockeys must carry assigned weights aboard each horse. If a jockey is assigned, for example, 116 pounds, there are three possibilities: 1) he weighs exactly 116; 2) he weighs less, in which case lead weights are inserted in the saddle pads to bring him up to that weight; or 3) he weighs more, in which case he is listed as an overweight. All overweights are shown on the tote board.

If the jockey in the above example were riding No. 4 in the first race and weighed in at 118 pounds, it would show on the tote board as: first race, No. 4, two pounds overweight.

Other changes can occur after the racing program has been printed, and those changes are shown on the tote board as well. They include things like scratches, jockey changes, medication changes, and use of special equipment. Bettors need to check the tote

---

TOTE BOARD TIPS

Before placing a bet, check the tote board or in-house TV monitors for:

• The race number (You don't want to bet on the wrong race!)

• Updated odds and mutuel pools

• Minutes to post (Don't wait so long you risk getting shut out!)

• Jockey changes and overweights

board constantly for those useful pieces of information.

Track Condition: The conditions of the dirt track and turf course are also listed on the tote board. You know that on a bright, sunny day when it has not rained for weeks that a dirt track will be listed as fast and a turf course as firm. But track condition becomes more important on bad weather days or on days after bad weather when the track may be rated "off" — good, sloppy, or muddy for a dirt track and good, soft, or yielding for a turf course. On "off" tracks, results may be less formful. Track and course conditions can even change during the course of a racing program. Rain during the day may change a track from fast to sloppy; winds may dry a track out and change it from muddy to good.

One can easily see why the most important piece of equipment at any racetrack is the tote board. Without it, patrons would have a hard time negotiating their way through an enjoyable day at the races.

By Dan Liebman

The Odds

The tote board, packed with constantly changing numbers, might seem intimidating, but understanding the odds it displays for each horse is fairly straightforward.

The odds can actually be thought about in terms of dollars; for instance, think of 2-1 odds as $2 profit for every $1 wagered, if your horse comes in. Let's say you wager $2 (the minimum bet at most tracks) on the number three horse, which goes off at 2-1 odds. If the number three horse wins, you will receive approximately $6 when you cash your ticket, a $4 return along with your original $2 bet.

Since the tote board reflects odds that have been rounded off and the payoff is based on the actual odds, which are usually rounded down to the nearest five-cent, ten-cent, or twenty-cent increment (called breakage), your payoff may be less than you expect.

To calculate the precise win odds on a horse, you need to look at some other figures on the tote board: the total win pool (all the money bet on all the horses to win) and the amount bettors have wagered on the particular horse that has caught your eye. But, before you can calculate the precise odds, you must subtract the track's "take" from the total win pool.

(Tracks usually take between 14 percent and 20 percent of a total pool to pay state and local taxes, purse money, and expenses, and to go toward the track's profit. The takeout for exotic bets is usually even higher.) After the take is subtracted from the total pool, subtract the total amount bet on your horse. To find the exact odds on your horse, take that sum and divide it by again using the total amount bet on your horse.

Here is an example:

Total win pool: $900
Take amount: 15 percent
Total amount bet on horse number three: $300

$900 - 15 percent = $765
$765 - $300 = $465
$465 / $300 = $1.55

Rounded off to $1.50 for breakage yields odds of 1.5 to 1, or 3-2 as it would appear on the tote board, which yields a payoff of $5 on a $2 wager.

Odds below even money return less than a dollar for every dollar wagered. For example, 3-5 means you receive $3 for every $5 wagered, or 60 cents for each dollar.

Place pools and show pools work the same way as win pools. Payoffs, though, for place and show bets are less than for win because the money in those pools has to be divided either twice for place (first-

PAYOFFS

ODDS	PAYS	ODDS	PAYS
1-5	$2.40	3-1	$8.00
2-5	$2.80	7-2	$9.00
1-2	$3.00	4-1	$10.00
3-5	$3.20	9-2	$11.00
4-5	$3.60	5-1	$12.00
1-1	$4.00	6-1	$14.00
6-5	$4.40	7-1	$16.00
7-5	$4.80	8-1	$18.00
3-2	$5.00	9-1	$20.00
8-5	$5.20	10-1	$22.00
9-5	$5.60	15-1	$32.00
2-1	$6.00	20-1	$42.00
5-2	$7.00	30-1	$62.00
		50-1	$102.00

and second-place horses) or three times for show (first-, second-, and third-place horses).

On rare occasions a horse will pay more to show than to win. This anomaly occurs when a betting crowd is so behind a horse that it is bet down to nothing to win and is overlooked in the show pool. Also, on rare occasions a minus pool can occur when an extremely heavily bet favorite wins and the track must payout more than it took in.

Exotic bets such as exactas, trifectas, and pick sixes also have their own pools, but, as mentioned before, tracks usually take more out from these pools. The odds for exotic bets, as well as for place and show bets, will not appear on the tote board but can be figured using the method discussed above. The tote board will show the total pools for win, place, and show bets, and the totals for the individual horses. The pools for exotic bets and probable payoffs can be better seen on closed-circuit television monitors

throughout the track.

Remember the odds change continually up until post time as bettors, including those at off-track betting locations, place their wagers. The pools include not only bets made at the track at which the race is run but also bets from hundreds of other simulcast locations and betting operations. A vast majority of the money bet on a race comes from outside the track. For example, Derby-goers at Churchill Downs in 2004 bet only $9.5 million of the $99 million total handle.

The pari-mutuel wagering system basically is a contest among bettors, with the track holding the stakes. The money bet in each of the pools is divided among those who have winning tickets.

Before the day's racing, a track betting expert sets the "morning line" that appears in the program and sometimes in the local newspaper. This morning line is based on how the track betting expert anticipates the public will bet; it is not based upon how the expert thinks the horse will fare. Once wagering begins, however, the amount of money actually bet on each horse determines the odds that are shown on the tote board and throughout the track on the closed-circuit television monitors.

The payoffs that appear after each race on the tote board are the $2 payoffs to win, place, and show. Payoffs on exactas, quinellas, trifectas, and pick threes are shown on the tote board following each race too, either the $2 payoff or the $1 payoff.

By Rena Baer

Types of Wagers

There are two general categories of wagers in Thoroughbred horse racing. The first is "straight" wagers. Straight wagers involve playing one horse in one race. The second category is "exotic" wagers. These wagers involve playing at least two horses in one race or across races.

Straight Wagers

Straight wagers are the easiest to make and understand, and they cover win, place, show, and head-to-head betting. Win, place, and show betting are offered on almost every race (on occasion due to a small field, show wagering may not be offered). Head-to-head wagering is usually offered on a selected race each day or between popular horses in stakes races. The minimum bet for these wagers is $2.

Let's take a look at each type of straight wager.

Win — Betting to win is probably the easiest wager to understand. Win betting is also referred

Placing a bet at a mutuel window.

to as placing a bet "on the nose." Your horse must finish first in the race for you to win or "cash" the bet. The win payoffs are easily determined by looking at the tote board (See Chapter 3; for payoffs chart, see Chapter 4.).

In general, on any given day at the races, the win payoffs will range between $3 and $40. The lowest possible win payoff is $2.20, and there is no limit on the largest possible payoff. Win betting is very popular among horseplayers. If there is a disadvantage to betting to win, of course, it is that your horse has to win to cash the ticket — losing by a nose only leaves you with thoughts of "woulda, coulda, shoulda ..."

Place — When you are betting to place, your horse must finish first or second for you to cash the wager. Place betting is a little more conservative than win betting and gives you a chance to be "mostly right" about a horse because your horse can finish first or second and you cash the bet. The place payoffs range between $2.40 and $12 during the average racing day. The lowest possible place payoff is $2.10 and there is no limit on the largest possible payoff. The disadvantage with place betting is that payoffs can be low and those payoffs are not easily determined in advance, because the payoffs vary,

33

depending on which two horses run first and second.

Show — Betting to show means your horse must finish first, second, or third for you to cash the wager. Show betting is the most conservative of straight betting as you are only betting your horse will finish "in the money" (first, second, or third). Show bets have a $2 minimum and in general payoffs will range between $2.10 and $8 on any given day at the races. The lowest possible payoff is $2.10, and there is no limit on the largest payoff. Similar to place payoffs, show payoffs tend to be very low, and you can't easily predict the payoffs because they are dependent on the top three finishers in the race.

In most cases, you won't be able to pay for a hot dog with $2 show betting. However, there are several unique situations where seasoned players may bet to show. The first situation is where both halves of an entry (two horses who are running as one for wagering purposes) could both finish in the money. If that does happen, the show payoff

may be higher than either the win or place payoff.

The second situation involves what are commonly called "bridge-jumpers." Bridge-jumpers are players who make large wagers on a heavily favored horse to show. These wagers can run into the hundreds of thousands of dollars and are usually on top-quality stakes horses that are racing against weak opposition in small fields. On occasion these horses run out of the money. When this happens, because the horse that had the large amount of money bet to show on it did not run first, second, or third, the show payoffs explode and the people who bet that large sum of money to show jokingly then go to a bridge (the higher, the better) and jump.

Head-to-Head Wagering — The final straight wager is a head-to-head wager. This bet is usually offered on one race a day at certain tracks and/or is offered in a big stakes race where two successful, well-known horses are racing against each other. To win the head-to-head bet, the horse you play must finish in front of the other horse against which it is matched. As long as the horse you bet finishes in front of the other horse, no matter where your horse finishes, you win. The disadvantage with this wager is that the payoffs tend to be low and under $4.

When first attending the races, most people will learn about making straight wagers before learning about making exotic wagers. There are some combinations of straight wagers that players will make on the way to learning about exotic wagers.

Some players will bet a horse to

PLACING A BET

Go to a mutuel clerk window with your bets prepared and money ready.

1. Name of the racetrack (if betting on a simulcast track)
2. The race number (ex: Race 5)
3. The amount of bet (ex: $2)
4. The type of bet (ex: Win)
5. The horse's post position number (ex: #4)

You would say, _"For Churchill Downs, race 5, I need $2 to Win on #4."_

Be sure and double check your ticket(s) before you walk away from the window!

win and place (WP). If your horse finishes first, you would cash both the win and place bet. If your horse finishes second, you would lose the win bet but cash the place bet. Other players will bet a horse "across the board." This bet refers to playing a horse to win, place, and show (WPS). If your horse finishes first, you would cash all three bets. If your horse finishes second, you would lose the win bet but cash the place and show bet. If your horse finishes third, you would lose the win and place bet but cash the show bet.

Summary

Years ago most betting options were primarily straight wagers. During the past three decades, straight wagers have lost their luster as racing fans chase the higher payoffs of exotic wagers. However, nothing is wrong with straight betting, and playing horses to win, place, and/or show gives you a good chance at cashing tickets while learning about handicapping and betting. In addition, many players lose sight of straight wagering (especially betting to win) in their quest to cash exotic wagers. No matter what level of handicapper you consider yourself, if you think a horse will win a race, betting to win should be your first option before considering exotic wagers.

Exotic Wagering

Now the fun begins. While straight wagering is easy to do and understand, exotic wagering can be a little more challenging. Fans flock to exotic wagers because their potential payoffs are high for a small investment. Exotic wagering also offers the opportunity to play races when straight betting isn't a good option because you like more than one horse in a race or the race has an evenly matched field. Finally, exotic wagering offers options when there is a heavy favorite who is a likely winner and betting to win is an unattractive option because of the low win payoff.

Exotic wagers include exactas, quinellas, trifectas, superfectas, daily doubles, pick threes, pick fours, pick fives, pick sixes, and win/place pick-alls. To find out what types of exotic wagers are offered on a particular race, check the program. Sometimes exotic wagering options on a race outnumber the horses running in the race! In most cases, the minimum bet for exotics is $1. The daily double, pick six, and quinellas are the exceptions where the minimum bet is usually $2.

Again, while understanding and making exotic wagers can be a little more complicated, the different types of exotics really are not that hard to understand. Let's look at each type of exotic wager.

Exotic Wagers Within a Race

Exactas

The exacta is one of the more popular exotic wagers. Exactas are offered on every race at most tracks. An exacta requires you to select the first two finishers of a race in exact order. For example, should the #4 win the race and #8 finish second, the exacta will pay to anyone who correctly bet a 4/8 exacta combination. Most players will play more than one exacta combination in a race. However, if you played only a 4/8 exacta and the finish was 4/8, this is called hitting it "cold" as you have played only one combination, the winning one.

Advantages: As with all exotic wagers, the exacta offers the opportunity to win large payoffs with small wagers.

Quick Strategies: You don't have to play just one straight exacta in a race in an attempt to hit that race cold. There are several options when playing exactas where you play more than one combination of horses in the race. By playing more combinations, you give yourself a better chance of winning the exacta. These strategies include boxing horses, playing wheels, or playing part-wheels.

Exacta Box — You box all possible combinations of the horses you like in a given race. You can box a minimum of two horses all the way up to boxing the entire field. You would want to play an exacta box when you like two or more horses in the race but don't really have an opinion favoring one over the others. A three-horse exacta box has six total wagers, which cover all combinations of those three horses.

For example, if you liked horses #2, #3, and #5, you could box them in the exacta. This bet would have six combinations (2/3, 2/5,

3/2, 3/5, 5/2, 5/3) and cost $6 based on the $1 minimum bet. For you to cash the bet, two of the horses you boxed must run first and second.

To make this wager, you would say to the teller "$1 exacta box 2, 3, 5." (Figure 1.)

The figures below show the cost of an exacta box with different numbers of horses based on a $1 minimum bet:

2-horse box = $2
3-horse box = $6
4-horse box = $12
5-horse box = $20
6-horse box = $30
7-horse box = $42
8-horse box = $56
9-horse box = $72
10-horse box = $90

As you can see, adding horses to an exacta box will greatly increase its cost. There are rare occasions when a five-, six-, or higher horse exacta box may be a good bet, but, in general, boxing four or more horses is a poor bet as you have lowered your potential return by spending so much to make the wager.

Exacta Part-Wheel — This type of wager plays one or more horses in combination with other horses in the race. There are many options when using a part-wheel, as shown in the following examples. You might want to play exacta part-wheels when you have an opinion favoring one or more horses to win and you like one or more horses to run second but not to win. If you use only one horse in either the win position (on top) or the second position (underneath) with all others

```
Aqueduct                              F4
02 Feb 05       1 RACE 2            1:35

    $1  EXB    2,3,5              $6.00

6 BETS            TOTAL           $6.00
         8FDF0-986EF-0A75D

OFFLINE---INVALID TICKET---OFFLINE
```

Figure 1. Exacta Box.

in a race, it is an exacta wheel.

Example #1: Let's say you like the #6 to win the race and think the #4, #8, and #10 could run second. To play an exacta that covers the #6 winning and either the #4, #8, and #10 running second, you would play an exacta part-wheel: 6/4-8-10. This bet would have three combina-

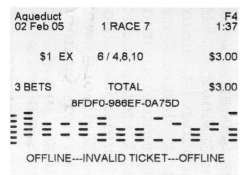

Figure 2. Exacta Part-Wheel.

tions (6/4, 6/8, and 6/10) and cost $3. To make this bet, you would say to the teller "$1 exacta part-wheel 6 with 4, 8, and 10." (Figure 2.)

For you to cash this ticket, the #6 must win the race and either the #4, #8, or #10 must finish second.

Continuing with this example, let's say you like the #6 to finish either first or second with those same contenders (4, 8, and 10). You could put the six on top (first) and then underneath (second) those contenders in two exacta part-wheels: 6/4-8-10, 4-8-10/6. This bet would have six combinations (6/4, 6/8, 6/10, 4/6, 8/6, 10/6) and cost $6. To make this bet, you would say to the teller "$1 exacta part-wheel 6 with 4, 8, 10 and 4, 8, 10 with the 6." Depending on the totalizator system your track is using, this bet could be made by saying "$1 exacta box 6 with 4, 8, 10."

Example #2: Let's say you like horses #3 and #4 as potential winners of a race and the #7 as a horse you think could run second. To play an exacta that covers horses #3 and #4 winning and/or running second and adding #7 also in second, you would play an exacta part-wheel: 3-4/3-4-7. This bet would have four combinations (3/4, 3/7, 4/3, 4/7) and cost $4. To make this bet, you would say to the teller "$1 exacta part-wheel 3, 4 with the 3, 4, and 7."

Should the final order of the race include any of these combinations, you would have a winning bet.

Example #3: Let's say you like the #7 to win the race in a ten-horse field but have no opinion on who will run second so you decide to use all the horses in the second position. This bet is an exacta wheel and would have nine different combinations: 7/all (7/1-2-3-4-5-6-8-9-10) and cost $9. To make this bet, you would say to the teller "$1 exacta wheel, 7 with all." (Figure 3.)

If the #7 wins the race, you win the exacta; the higher the odds on the second-place finisher, the higher your payoff.

Figure 3. Exacta Wheel.

Quinellas

Quinella wagering requires you to select the top two finishers in a race, but you don't have to pick the exact order of finish. Quinellas are very similar to exactas but are not as popular, and many racetracks do not offer quinella wagering. Again as with exactas, you are trying to predict the top two finishers in a race. For example, if you played a 1-5 quinella you would win if #1 won the race and the #5 finished second or if the #5 won the race and the #1 finished second. In most cases, the minimum bet is $2.

Advantages: Quinellas offer the potential of decent payoffs with smaller wager amounts and without having to pick the exact order of finish.

Quick Strategies: Quinella wagering is very similar to exacta wagering and strategies include boxing, part-wheeling, and wheeling.

Quinella Box — Quinella boxes are playing all possible combinations of the horses you like in a given race. You can play a minimum of two horses in a quinella and box as many as the entire field. A four-horse quinella box would have six total wagers and cover all possible combinations of those four horses.

For example, if you wanted to box #3, #4, #8, and #9 in the quinella, you would have six combinations (3/4, 3/8, 3/9, 4/8, 4/9, 8/9) for a total of $12 (based on the $2 minimum bet). For you to cash the bet, one of your combinations must have the top two, but remember, they do not have to finish in exact order. Should the #8 win the race and the #3 run second, you would have a winning quinella as the exact finish position does not matter.

To make this wager, you would say to the teller "$2 quinella box 3, 4, 8, and 9." (Figure 4.)

Here is a table showing the cost of quinella boxes with different numbers of horses based on a $2 minimum bet:

2-horse = $2	7-horse = $42
3-horse = $6	8-horse = $56
4-horse = $12	9-horse = $72
5-horse = $20	10-horse = $90
6-horse = $30	

Quinella Part-Wheel — This wager plays one or more horses in a race in combination with other horses in a race. There are many options when using quinella part-wheels. Below are two examples.

Example #1: Let's say you think the #6 horse will run first or second in a race and you think the #3 and #5 are its primary competition. To play a quinella for this race, you would play a quinella part-wheel: 6/3-5. This bet would have two combinations (3/6, 5/6) and cost $4. You would win if the race finished 6-3, 6-5, 3-6, or 5-6. To make this bet, you would say to the teller "$2 quinella part-

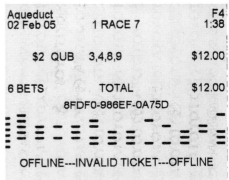

Aqueduct   F4
02 Feb 05   1 RACE 7   1:38

$2 QUB 3,4,8,9 $12.00

6 BETS   TOTAL $12.00
   8FDF0-986EF-0A75D

OFFLINE---INVALID TICKET---OFFLINE

Figure 4. Quinella Box.

wheel 6 with 3, 5."

Example #2: Let's say you like the #1 horse to run first or second in an eight-horse field and you have no other opinion in the race and want to use all in the quinella. To play a quinella in this race, you would play a quinella wheel: 1 with all (2, 3, 4, 5, 6, 7, 8). This bet would have seven combinations (1/2, 1/3, 1/4, 1/5, 1/6, 1/7, 1/8) and cost $14. To make this bet, you would say to the teller "$2 quinella wheel 1 with all."

As long as the #1 horse runs first or second, you are guaranteed a winning ticket as you have played all with the #1. In this case by wheeling, you are hoping for a longshot to run with the #1 horse.

Trifectas

Trifectas are another of the more popular exotic wagers. This wager requires you to select the first three finishers of a race in the exact order. For example, should the #9 win the race, #6 finish second, and #2 finish third, the winning trifecta will be anyone who played a 9/6/2 trifecta ticket. Trifectas are offered on most races but not all, as a minimum number of horses in a race may be needed to offer the trifecta. This minimum number will vary from state to state.

Advantages: The potential for nice, sometimes huge, payoffs with limited amount wagered.

Quick Strategies: Options for playing trifectas include boxing, part-wheeling, and wheeling. Because of the nature of trifecta wagering, be aware that adding horses to boxes or part-wheels can increase your wager dramatically. For example

(see table on page 40), a $1 four-horse trifecta box costs $24, but a five-horse trifecta box costs $60. To avoid the substantial increase in costs when adding horses, most players will break down their selections to "key" horses and "marginal horses." Key horses are horses the player thinks have the best chance of winning and/or running well. Marginal horses are horses the player thinks have a good chance of running second or third but not winning the race.

Trifecta Box — This wager plays all possible combinations of all the horses you like in a given race. You can box a minimum of three horses all the way to boxing the entire field. A $1 three-horse trifecta box has six total wagers, which cover all combinations of those three horses.

For example, if you wanted to box #2, #6, and #8 in the trifecta, this bet has six combinations (2/6/8, 2/8/6, 6/2/8, 6/8/2, 8/6/2, 8/2/6) and a total cost of $6. To

```
Aqueduct                              F4
02 Feb 05        1 RACE 7          1:38

      $1  TRIB   2,6,8            $6.00

6 BETS            TOTAL           $6.00
            8FDF0-986EF-0A75D

   OFFLINE---INVALID TICKET---OFFLINE
```

Figure 5. Trifecta Box.

cash the bet, the order of the top three finishers must be one of those six combinations.

To make this wager, you would say to the teller "$1 trifecta box 2, 6, 8." (Figure 5.)

Below is a table showing the

costs of a trifecta box with different numbers of horses based on a $1 minimum bet:

3-horse box = $6
4-horse box = $24
5-horse box = $60
6-horse box = $120
7-horse box = $210
8-horse box = $336
9-horse box = $504
10-horse box = $720

Again, adding horses to trifecta boxes can greatly increase the cost of the trifecta box, and most players will use trifecta part-wheels to avoid these increased costs.

Trifecta Part-Wheel — This wager plays one or more key horses with other contenders in the race. Just like playing exactas, there are several options when using part-wheels as you can see in the examples below. If you use only one horse in the first position with all others in a race, it is called a trifecta wheel.

Example #1: Let's say you like the #5 to win the race and feel there are three other horses you would like to use underneath the #5 to finish second and third. Those horses are the #1, #2, and #4. A trifecta part-wheel using those horses would be the following: 5/1-2-4/1-

2-4. This bet would have six combinations (5/1/2, 5/2/1, 5/1/4, 5/4/1, 5/2/4, 5/4/2) and cost $6 ($1 minimum bet). To make this bet, you would say to the teller "$1 trifecta part-wheel 5 with the 1, 2, 4."

You would have a winning ticket if the final order of finish included one of those combinations.

Example #2: Let's say you like the #6 and #8 and think either could win the race. You think the #7 could sneak between those horses for second and you would like to throw in the #1 and #3 for third as longshot possibilities (marginal horses). At this point, since you like a total of five horses as potential finishers in the top three, boxing all five in the trifecta would cost $60. However, you can make a wager using the marginal horses underneath (second or third) by playing a trifecta part-wheel and not spend $60.

To play this race using a trifecta part-wheel, you would play #6 and #8 in the first position, #6, #7 and #8 in the second position and #1, #3, #6, #7, and #8 in the third position. This part-wheel looks like this: 6-8/6-7-8/1-3-6-7-8. This bet would have twelve combinations (6/7/1, 6/7/3, 6/7/8, 6/8/1, 6/8/3, 6/8/7, 8/7/1, 8/7/3, 8/7/6, 8/6/1, 8/6/3, 8/6/7) and cost $12 based on a $1 minimum bet. To make this bet, you would say to the teller "$1 trifecta part-wheel 6, 8 with the 6, 7, 8 with the 1, 3, 6, 7, 8." (Figure 6.)

Again, you are using the part-wheel option to play the race according to your handicapping opinion and also giving yourself a decent chance of winning the bet if you are right, without spending the large amount of

```
Aqueduct                           F4
02 Feb 05        1 RACE 7       1:39

   $1  TRI     6,8 / 6,7,8 / 1,3,6,
                7,8                $12.00

12 BETS          TOTAL           $12.00
        8FDF0-986EF-0A75D


    OFFLINE---INVALID TICKET---OFFLINE
```

Figure 6. Trifecta Part-Wheel.

money to box all the horses you like. The above examples are just a couple of unlimited potential trifecta part-wheels you can make.

Superfectas

Superfectas have grown in popularity over the past few years and require you to select the first four finishers of a race in exact order. Superfectas are usually offered on selected races throughout the day; check your program to see which races offer superfecta betting. The superfecta is really just a "super-sized" trifecta. For example, should the #3 win the race, #6 finish second, #10 finish third, and #1 finish fourth, a winning superfecta ticket would have that 3/6/10/1 combination.

Advantages: Of all the exotic wagers offered on a race (exactas, quinellas, trifectas), this bet has the potential for the largest payoffs — regularly paying tens or even hundreds of thousands of dollars.

Quick Strategies: As mentioned, the superfecta is a super-sized trifecta and the same strategies apply in regard to boxing, part-wheeling, and wheeling. Also, just as with the trifecta, adding additional horses greatly increases the cost of the bet, so most players will concentrate their wagering around one or two key horses and play marginal horses underneath.

Superfecta Boxes — This wager allows you to play all possible combinations of the horses you like. You can box a minimum of four horses all the way up to boxing the entire field. A four-horse superfecta box has a total of 24 wagers, which cover all combinations of those four horses. For example, if you

wanted to box horses #1, #5, #7, and #9 in the superfecta, this bet would have 24 combinations (including 1/5/7/9, 5/7/1/9, 9/1/7/5, and so on) and cost $24 (based on a $1 minimum bet). In order for you to cash the bet, your four picks must run first, second, third, and fourth in any order. To make this wager, you would say to the teller "$1 superfecta box 1, 5, 7, and 9." (Figure 7.)

```
Aqueduct                              F4
02 Feb 05        1 RACE 7           1:39

     $1  SPRB  1,5,7,9             $24.00

24 BETS           TOTAL           $24.00
          8FDF0-986EF-0A75D

   OFFLINE---INVALID TICKET---OFFLINE
```

Figure 7. Superfecta Box.

Below is a table that shows the cost of a superfecta box with different numbers of horses based on a $1 minimum bet.

4-horse box = $24
5-horse box = $120
6-horse box = $360
7-horse box = $840
8-horse box = $1,680

Superfecta Part-Wheel — This wager plays one or more key horses with other contenders in the race. If you use only one horse in the first position with all other horses in second, third, and fourth, it is called a superfecta wheel.

Obviously, coming up with a winning superfecta ticket is not easy — it can be hard enough to pick the winner of a race, so picking the exact order down to fourth place is as tough as it gets. Some players will try to bet small amounts on superfectas, such as playing three or four $1 straight superfecta tickets since boxes or wheels can be very expensive. Of course, they could win, but successful players will approach this wager by narrowing the field down to key horses and marginal horses and then playing combinations of those horses.

Superfectas are potentially a very good bet in races where you have a strong opinion that leaves you with one or two key horses and a few marginal horses. There are ways to play superfectas in races such as this where you give yourself a decent chance of winning at a reasonable cost by using a part-wheel. Here are two examples.

Example #1: Let's say you like the #6 to win the race and feel there are four other horses you would like to use underneath the #6 to complete the second-, third-, and fourth-place positions. Those horses are #1, #7, #8, and #9. To play a superfecta using these horses underneath the #6, you would place a $1 superfecta part-wheel: 6/1-7-8-9/1-7-8-9/1-7-8-9. This bet would have 24 combinations (6/1/7/8, 6/1/7/9, 6/1/8/7, 6/1/8/9, 6/1/9/7, 6/1/9/8, 6/7/1/8, 6/7/1/9, 6/7/8/1, etc.) and cost $24. To make this bet, you would say to the teller "$1 superfecta part-wheel 6 with the 1, 7, 8, 9."

If the race finish included any one of those combinations, you would have a winning ticket.

Example #2: Let's say you like the #3 and #5 as potential winners of the race. In addition, you think the #7 has a good chance to run well (at best finish second) and you feel the #4 and #6 could sneak into

third and the #9 likes running fourth, so you want to put him fourth only. At this point if you wanted to box all six horses (3, 4, 5, 6, 7, and 9) in a superfecta box, it would cost you $360. But, you can play a part-wheel, which places horses in certain positions based on your opinion of those horses. For this bet, a part-wheel would look like this: 3-5/3-5-7/3-4-5-6-7/3-4-5-6-7-9. This bet would have 36 combinations and cost $36. To make this bet, you would say to the teller "$1 superfecta part-wheel 3, 5 with 3, 5, 7 with 3, 4, 5, 6, 7 with 3, 4, 5, 6, 7, 9."

If the final order of finish included one of those combinations, you would have a winning ticket.

The Math

One area we have skipped over in discussing exacta, trifecta, superfecta boxes, and part-wheels is how to calculate the cost of each ticket. Once you get the hang of it, figuring the costs of those tickets is not hard and can be very useful in figuring out how much you are going to be spending before you bet. The costs of boxing horses in the exactas, quinellas, trifectas, and superfectas have been listed in the tables in each section. Of course, there aren't tables available for part-wheels as part-wheels can include any number of horses.

There are two ways to calculate the costs of any exotic wager. The easiest way is to walk up to a SAM (screen activated machine), or self-betting machine, at any track and punch in the ticket and the cost will be shown on the screen. You can also do this if you are betting online as many sites offer online wagering calculators. The other way is to figure out the cost for each type of wager by hand. Below are some examples of how to figure the costs of each type of bet. As you follow along, figuring the cost by hand should become easier .

Exacta Box: If you are playing four horses in an exacta box, you have four potential winners of the race. For you to win the bet, one of your horses must win the race; you would then have three potential horses that could run second. So, you have four potential winners and three potential second-place finishes. The cost of a four-horse exacta box is 4 x 3, or 12 times the amount of the bet you would like to make. If you play a $1 exacta box, the cost would be $12 (12 x $1). If you played a $3 exacta box, the cost would be $36 (12 x $3). The math would be similar for two-horse exacta boxes, three-horse exacta boxes, five-horse and up exacta boxes. A six-horse exacta box would be 6 x 5, or 30 times the amount of your bet, a seven-horse exacta box would be 7 x 6, or 42 times the amount of your bet and so on.

Exacta Part-Wheel: Let's say you would like to play an exacta part-wheel 3-4/3-4-5-6. To figure the cost of this bet, you first determine

THE BLOOD-HORSE

Do the math to plan your bets better.

how many horses you have in the win position — in this case two (3, 4). You then figure how many horses you have in the second position, in this case four (3, 4, 5, and 6). However, for you to win the bet, one of your horses (the 3 or 4) must win the race, leaving you with only three potential second-place finishers. So you have two potential winners and three potential second-place finishers. The cost of this exacta part-wheel is 2 x 3, or 6 times the amount of your bet — if you bet a $1 exacta part-wheel, the cost would be $6. If you bet a $3 exacta part-wheel, the cost would be $18.

Trifecta Box: This follows the same calculations as the exacta box; only we are adding one more position, third place. For example, if you play a five-horse trifecta box, you have five potential winners of the race. Of course, for your bet to be successful, one of those five horses has to win, leaving you with four potential second-place finishers. Again, for you to win the bet, one of your horses has to win, but one also has to run second, leaving you with three potential third-place finishers. So, in a five-horse trifecta box, you have five potential winners, four potential second-place finishers, and three potential third-place finishers. The cost is 5 x 4 x 3, or 60 times the amount of the bet you would like to make.

A $1 five-horse trifecta box would cost $60 (60 x $1). A $3 five-horse trifecta box would cost $180 (60 x $3). The math behind other boxes is the same. A six-horse trifecta box is 6 x 5 x 4, or 120 times the amount of your bet. A seven-horse trifecta box is 7 x 6 x 5, or 210 times the amount of your bet and so on and so on.

Trifecta Part-Wheel: Let's say you want to figure the cost of a trifecta part-wheel 1-2/1-2-5/1-2-5-6-7. To figure the cost of this bet, your first question is how many horses are in the first position, in this case two (1, 2). The next question is how many horses are you using in the second position, in this case three (1, 2, and 5). However, for you to win the bet, one of your horses has to win (either the 1 or 2) leaving you with two potential second-place finishers. The last question is how many horses are you using in the third position, in this case five (1, 2, 5, 6, 7).

However, for you to win the bet, one of your horses has to win and another must come in second, leaving you with three potential third-place finishers. So you have two potential winners, two potential second-place finishers, and three potential third-place finishers. The cost of this trifecta part-wheel is 2 x 2 x 3, or 12 times the amount of your bet. If you did a $1 trifecta part-wheel, the cost would be $12 (12 x $1). If you did a $3 trifecta part-wheel, the cost would be $36 (12 x $3).

Superfecta boxes and part-wheels are figured the same way as exacta and trifecta boxes, you are just adding a fourth-place position.

Exotic Wagers Across Several Races

In addition to exotic wagers in any one race, several exotic wagers involve two or more races. These include the daily double, pick three, pick four, pick five, pick six, and win/place pick-alls. In all cases

except one (the win/place pick-all), these wagers involve picking winners of races. Of course, these wagers must be made before the first race in the series (each race is called a "leg") and all but the pick six and daily double have a minimum $1 bet. The pick six and daily double have a $2 minimum bet; however, some tracks allow a $1 daily double bet.

Daily Double

The daily double is probably the oldest, most recognized, and traditional of the exotic wagers. To win the daily double, you must select the winner of two consecutive races. For example, should the #6 win the first race and #10 win the second race, the winning daily double will be 6/10. Most tracks

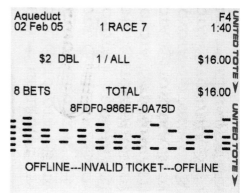

Figure 8. Daily Double Wheel.

will have an early daily double on the first two races and a late daily double on the last two races. Some tracks have "rolling" daily doubles. This is where a daily double begins in the first race and a new one starts with each race until the last two races on the card.

Advantages: As with all exotics, there is potential for large payoffs with small wagers. Also, you are dealing with picking winners of races unlike exactas, trifectas, and superfectas where you a trying to pick horses that run second, third, and/or fourth.

Quick Strategies: The most common strategy in playing the daily double is to identify one key horse (called a "single") and then play combinations using that single with contenders in the other leg. This strategy is also used in playing pick threes, pick fours, pick fives, and pick sixes. The other strategy is to play all combinations of the horses you like in each leg. Of course, you can play a cold or "straight" daily double by selecting one horse in each race.

Daily Double Wheel — This wager plays one horse in one of the daily double races and uses all of the horses in the other leg of the daily double.

For example, let's say you like the #1 to win the first race of the day, and you would like to use all the horses in the second race (e.g., an eight horse field). To make this wager, you would play a daily double wheel: 1/1-8. This bet would have eight combinations (1/1, 1/2, 1/3, 1/4, 1/5, 1/6, 1/7, 1/8) and cost $16. You would win if the #1 was the winner of the first race. To make this bet you would say to the teller "$2 daily double wheel, #1 with all." (Figure 8.)

Daily Double Part-Wheel — This wager plays one or more horses in one of the daily double races and uses one or more horses in the other leg of the daily double.

For example, let's say you like both the #1 and #3 as potential winners of the first race and horses #4, #6, and #10 as potential winners of the second race. To play

Figure 9. Daily Double Part-Wheel.

these combinations of horses for the daily double, you would play a daily double part-wheel: 1-3/4-6-10. This bet would have six combinations (1/4, 1/6, 1/10, 3/4, 3/6, 3/10) and cost $12. You would win if any of these combinations came in. To make this bet, you would say to the teller "$2 daily double part-wheel 1, 3 with 4, 6, and 10." (Figure 9.)

Pick Three

The pick three has probably replaced the daily double as the most popular wager across races. You must select the first-place finisher of three straight races to win. Most tracks have "rolling" pick threes that start in the first race and continue till the last three races. Other tracks have pick threes starting with selected races. Check your program to see which races offer pick threes. The minimum bet for the pick three is $1.

Advantages: Pick threes can offer very nice payoffs, especially if you are able to beat a heavy favorite or series of favorites in the pick three.

Quick Strategies: Of course, you can play a "straight" pick three, selecting one horse in each leg. As mentioned when talking about the daily double, most players will play pick threes where they try to find a "single" in at least one of the pick three legs and use more than one horse in the other races. If you have a single, you can concentrate your betting around that one horse and spread your options in the other races, hoping to catch a longshot, especially if you think the favorites in those other races are vulnerable. Other strategies include playing all combinations of the horses you like in each leg.

Pick Three Part-Wheels — You can use this wager when you play one or more horses in each leg to one or more horses in the other legs. For example, let's say you like the #1 and #2 in the first leg, the #3, #4, and #5 in the second leg and the #6 in the final leg of the pick three. To play these combinations, you would play a pick three: 1-2/3-4-5/6. This wager would have six combinations (1/3/6, 1/4/6, 1/5/6, 2/3/6, 2/4/6, 2/5/6) and cost $6. You would win if any of those combinations came in. To make this bet, you would say to the teller "$1 pick three part-wheel 1, 2 with 3, 4, 5 with 6." (Figure 10.)

Again, the pick three is one of the most popular wagers across races. In addition to playing pick three part-wheels, you can vary the amounts of each part-wheel based on your view toward the race.

For example, let's take the above example ($1 pick three: 1-2/3-4-5/6) and break it up. Let's say you really like the #1 in the first leg but want to use the #2 as a backup. You then might play one pick three part-wheel for a $1 with the #2 (2/3-4-5/6), which costs $3

and then a $3 pick three (1/3-4-5/6), which would cost $9. You are varying the amounts played according to your opinion.

Another option is to play pick threes using a key horse with several horses in the other legs and a backup horse with a few horses in those other legs. Let's again say you really like the #1 horse in the first leg of a pick three but also want to use the #2 as a backup. In this example, however, instead of varying the wager amounts, you want to use the #2 as a backup with some of the main contenders in the next two legs and you want to spread your options even more in those legs when using the #1.

Sticking with the above example, you still feel the main contenders in the next leg are the #3, #4, and #5, but you wouldn't mind playing an "all" once, and you still like #6 in the final leg. To play a pick three according to your opinion, you would play one pick three part-wheel: 1-2/3-4-5/6, cost $6, and a second pick three part-wheel: 1/all/6 (which would cost $8 if the second leg has eight horses). Now, if you are right about the #1 winning the first leg, you will be alive to an "all" in the second leg and also have #3, #4, and #5 twice to

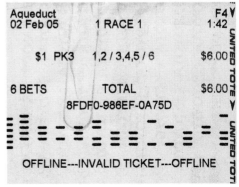

Figure 10. Pick Three Part-Wheel.

the #6 in the final leg. If you are partially right about the first leg and get the #2 to win, you would still have a chance at hitting the pick three.

Pick three betting can be a lot of fun, and the potential for huge payoffs is excellent. Experimenting and coming up with different strategies when playing the pick three (don't play each pick three exactly the same) will improve your success as a bettor.

Pick Four, Pick Five

The pick four/five bets are just extensions of the pick three, and the same advantages and strategies apply. For the pick four, you must select the winner of four consecutive races. Not every track offers a pick four, but some tracks now offer two pick fours. Check your program to see when this wager is offered.

With a pick five, the newest exotic wager, you must select the winner of five consecutive races. Check your program to see whether the pick five is offered at your track.

Pick Six

The pick six is the "Holy Grail" of horse race betting. You must select the winners of six consecutive races. The pick six has a $2 minimum bet and is offered at many racetracks, but it is most popular in southern California where the pools can reach millions of dollars.

There are two payoffs for the pick six. If at least one person has selected all six winners, there will be a pick six payoff. In addition, those who picked five of the six winners will get what is called a "consolation payoff." If no one picked six winners, those with the

SIMULCASTING

A simulcast is a live television transmission of a race to other tracks, off-track betting facilities, or other wagering outlets. *For example:* You are at the Fair Grounds in New Orleans betting on live races from Calder in Florida, Oaklawn in Arkansas, and Turfway Park in Kentucky.

next highest amount of winners (most likely five) will get the consolation payoff and the pick six will carryover to the next day. A two-day carryover at a southern California track can generate nationwide interest and draw large crowds to the races and simulcast facilities.

The best two-day carryovers occur when no one hits the pick six over the weekend. Having two days off (Mondays and Tuesdays usually being "dark days" at southern California tracks) to study the races and make a stop at the bank, everyone concentrates on Wednesday's card, generating a lot of excitement.

Advantages: The pick six has the potential for the largest payoff, sometimes life-changing payoffs in the hundreds of thousands and even millions of dollars.

Quick Strategies: As with other exotic wagering across several races, finding at least one, two, or even three "singles" is the goal of most players, which enables them to put more horses in other races in the hopes of catching a longshot that other bettors didn't play, knocking those bettors out.

Additionally, finding singles helps keep the cost of a pick six ticket reasonable. Another successful strategy is for players to identify key horses and "back-up" horses. The player would play more than one pick six ticket, covering different possibilities. (See the example below.) Pick six pay-offs can explode after one or more heavy favorites are beaten. Some players will pool their money and form a "pick six syndicate" to give themselves a better chance of winning as they will be able to spend more money and use more horses in the tougher races.

Example: Let's say you want to play the pick six. In most cases, the pick six will be offered on the last six races on the card, for this example races four through nine. First, here is your hypothetical opinion on each race:

Race #4: You like two horses here, the #5 and the #7.

Race #5: You think the #1 cannot lose.

Race #6: You feel the #6 is fairly strong, but horses #2 and #3 could upset.

Race #7: You are kind of lost here and want to use four horses, #3, #5, #6, and #8.

Race #8: You would like to use two horses in this race, #6 and #7.

Race #9: The #10 looks pretty strong here, but you give decent shots to #3 and #4.

Based on your opinion, you would probably want to play two separate pick six tickets. These tickets would be keyed around the #1 horse winning the second leg (race #5) and being right about one of your two stronger opinions — either the #6 in the sixth race or #10 in the ninth race as you will be using the back-ups on alternating tickets.

Let's break this down further. Look at the table above showing your key horses and back-ups. Here are the two tickets you should construct:

	KEY HORSE(S)	BACK-UP HORSE(S)
Race 4	5,7	
Race 5	1	
Race 6	6	2,3
Race 7	3,5,6,8	
Race 8	6,7	
Race 9	10	3,4

Ticket #1: 5-7/1/2-3-6/3-5-6-8/6-7/10, this ticket would cost $96.

Ticket #2: 5-7/1/6/3-5-6-8/6-7/3-4, this ticket would cost $48.

If you played one big ticket using all the horses you like (5-7/1/2-3-6/3-5-6-8/6-7/3-4-10), the cost would be $288. Instead, you have played two tickets according to your opinion of the races and have given yourself a reasonable chance at winning without spending $288. By the way, if you miss one race, you still are alive for five — the consolation payoff.

Win/Place Pick-All

This wager requires the bettor to select the horses that finish either first or second in all of the day's races. The minimum bet for this wager is $1, and it is offered at a few tracks. The biggest difference from this wager over the pick fours, fives, or sixes is that your horse does not have to win each race, just finish at least second.

The Math

The math behind figuring the costs of playing daily doubles, pick threes, fours, fives, sixes, and win/place pick-alls is much easier than the math behind exacta, trifecta, and superfecta wheels, boxes, and part-wheels. You just take the number of horses in each race and multiply them together and use that total times the amount of the bet.

For example, if you are playing a pick three part-wheel: 4-5/1-5-6/2-7-8, you have two horses in the first leg (4, 5), three horses in the second leg (1, 5, 6), and three horses in the final leg (2, 7, 8). The cost is 2 x 3 x 3, or 18 times the amount of your bet. If you play a $1 pick three, the cost would be $18 (18 x $1). If you played a $3 pick three, the cost would be $54 (18 x $3).

The math behind the daily doubles, pick fours, fives, sixes, or win/place pick-alls is the same — multiply together the number of horses you are using in each leg. One last note about the math behind exotic wagering. The more proficient you become at it, the better your chance at success. The last thing you want to do is go up to the window, call out a trifecta part-wheel you think is going to cost $18 and find out it costs $48. Practice using the SAM machines or online wagering calculators. Also, don't be intimidated. If you aren't sure of the costs of a wager, go to a mutuel clerk when there isn't a long line and ask for help to figure the cost.

Summary

As has been mentioned many times, exotic wagering offers the potential for large payoffs with minimal investments. Winning a large-paying exotic is part of the fun of betting on the races. But, there are a few things that you should be aware of when playing exotics.

Be prepared to have your horse(s) run well in a race but not have the exact winning combination. For example, you could be playing a superfecta part-wheel, be right about the top three finishers (which in itself isn't easy), and miss fourth place thereby losing everything. That is the nature of exotic wagering, and playing exotics such as the superfecta and pick six are not for the faint of heart. It is possible you could win or lose hundreds of thousands of dollars on a head-bob.

THE BLOOD-HORSE

Bettors make their choices on pick six ballots.

What do you do if you have a winning ticket?

After the race is made official (the "Official" sign will light up on the tote board) and payoffs are posted, just go to any mutuel clerk window and present your ticket or use a self-betting machine to get your money.

I will give you an example of a recent pick six loss I suffered at Santa Anita. I was five for five heading into the final race of the pick six. In that final race, I had two horses, a heavily favored 3-5 shot and the second choice. While many others felt the 3-5 shot was a stone cold lock, I had used another horse, just in case, as bad racing luck is always a possibility when playing any race. I felt I had the race covered in case the 3-5 shot had something go wrong by using another horse, the second choice. In fact, if the second choice were to win, I would probably cash a five-figure payoff. Of course, just like everyone else, I know I can lose any bet, but I felt as confident as I could going into this final race as my two choices towered over the field in ability; the rest of the field just could not run. The field was loaded and the gate opened. After about three strides, the 3-5 shot stumbled badly and threw his rider into the path of the other horse I had, the second choice. The rider of the second choice then took up his horse sharply to avoid the thrown rider of the 3-5 shot, losing several lengths and any chance.

So, four strides out of the gate, one of my horses was riderless and the other was far behind the field — thank you, sir, may I have another. Again, outcomes such as this occur on occasion when you are playing exotic wagers as you will miss out on big payoffs by head-bobs, bad racing luck, and any number of other scenarios that can happen during a horse race. Of course, you also can make huge scores when things go your way, which is one of the key attractions of exotic wagering.

Don't make the two most common mistakes players make regarding exotics. The first is playing equal amounts on horses that have different chances. For example, if you are boxing three horses in the exacta, the cost is $6. If you add one more horse to that box, you are spending $12. You have to ask yourself, is that additional horse really worth $6 more? You are doubling the cost of the ticket by adding one more horse, a horse you think is a possibility but really don't like as much as the other horses.

The second mistake most players make is spreading their money around by wheeling horses, hoping for a longshot. Of course, there are times when wheeling a horse is the thing to do, but wheeling just for the sake of wheeling in most cases is a waste of money.

As you learn about each type of exotic wager and as your attendance at the track increases and you make more and more exotic wagers, you will get comfortable in playing those wagers, which should lead to more opportunity to be successful and, more importantly, more fun. Good luck!

By John Lindley

The Psychology of Betting

As you become more and more familiar with wagering, especially wagering on exotics, you will experience tough losses and close calls. You may find one of the keys to being successful and also enjoying the races is to deal with those tough losses without letting them affect your decisions later in the day. Also, losing and winning streaks are inevitable aspects of gambling. These streaks could be due to luck (good or bad), good or bad handicapping or wagering decisions, or many other factors. In addition to your own experiences, at the track you will hear story after story of tough losses and near misses. Of course, you will also hear stories of great successes. However, most of the time people tend to dwell on their tough or unlucky losses.

Many talented handicappers are unable to win consistently because they are not emotionally able to handle tough losses or deal with losing streaks. This inability leads to bad decisions, for example after a tough loss. Or this might lead to a "can't win" attitude. However, taking certain steps prior to experiencing these swings associated with gambling may help you avoid a losing streak or handle a tough loss.

First, be prepared before you start your day at the track. Handicap before the races begin so as to have some idea of which races/horses you are going to bet. There are many distractions at the track. For example, prior to each race you have a post parade to watch, payoffs to analyze, bets to plan, and conversations with other horseplayers, etc. If you are somewhat prepared, you won't feel rushed or be forced to make last-minute decisions, which are recipes for bad decisions. Also, take enough money to last the day. Don't count

on winning your first few bets, so make sure you have enough money to play the later races if you do lose early. Many people expect they are going to win early and when that doesn't happen, they don't have enough money to play the later races, races they may have handicapped correctly. They become even more frustrated as those later selections win and they didn't have enough to bet them.

POINTS TO REMEMBER

For a good betting experience:
1. Be prepared before the races — and betting — begin.
2. Be consistent in your betting.
3. Expect bad luck from time to time.
4. Learn from your mistakes.

Second, be consistent in your wagering. Again, most people expect to win their first few bets, and, if they do, they may then increase their betting in the next few races. Or the opposite, if they lose their first few bets, they will bet

BARBARA D. LIVINGSTON

Remember: There's no such thing as a sure thing.

less in the next races. Instead try to be fairly consistent when playing each race. This isn't meant to tell you to bet the exact same amount on each race, but don't let those amounts depend on whether you won your last bet or whether you are losing or winning for the day. As mentioned in the previous paragraph, you should plan for losses as you probably are going to lose a majority of your bets.

Third, expect bad luck. In other words, you should know in advance that you may have the best horse but something unexpected can happen during the race and that horse gets beat. That is part of horse racing. At times you will encounter good luck and cash a wager that you probably should have lost and vice versa. Remember that all gambling includes some degree of luck, and don't let the times when bad luck strikes influence the decisions you make later in the day.

Fourth, learn from your mistakes. One of the factors that leads to a losing streak obviously is making mistakes. This could be over-looking or ignoring a certain horse or handicapping the race right but not betting it right. It is impossible to avoid making these mistakes, as that is part of the learning process. However, these mistakes can be used to your advantage if you learn from them. Review what you have done each day and identify where you made mistakes. There will be days where you are able to identify mistakes; other days you may conclude that you did everything right but just got beat. However, when you do identify past mistakes, you can learn from them and avoid making them in the future.

The above paragraphs listed some steps you can take to deal with those tough losses or a losing streak. Part of a successful player's skills is an ability to deal with the emotional ups and down associated with any gambling. That doesn't mean you shouldn't get mad after an unlucky loss due to a bad ride, or that you shouldn't celebrate after a big win. But take the good and bad in stride, stay consistent, and have fun.

By John Lindley

PART II

Handicapping Factors

Post Positions

In the 1982 Kentucky Derby, Gato Del Sol came away from the gate and settled into his usual position — at the rear of the field. Down the backstretch, he moved up along the outside. Through the turn for home, he took command, surging to the lead before the furlong pole in the one and a quarter-mile race. He flew under the finish wire two and a half lengths in front to win the world's most prestigious race.

The name Gato Del Sol is forever etched in racing lore, painted on the façade at Churchill Downs along with the names of 130 other horses to have worn the garland of roses. That he had post position eighteen in the nineteen-horse field was of little importance. In fact, few even remember that detail about the gray son of Cougar II.

What if Gato Del Sol had broken from post three instead of eighteen and had to settle off the lead group instead? And what if Cupecoy's Joy, who had speed and needed the lead, had broken from post eighteen instead of post one and couldn't have gotten to the front as he did? Would the outcome have been different?

Possibly.

No one can predict the future, nor can anyone rewrite history. So, too, with the outcome of a horse race. It is the kind of discussion that makes for, well, a good discussion. Nothing more; nothing less. But handicappers love to debate

Gato Del Sol (arrow) broke from the next-to-outside post to win the Derby.

ANNE M. EBERHARDT

Post position can affect a horse's initial placement in a race.

races after their conclusion, and post position is one of the things that often come up.

Post position is what stall in the starting gate a horse occupies. Is it important? Of course it is. It is one of the main factors, such as track condition, field size, race distance, etc., to consider when handicapping any race. But can post positions have absolutely no bearing whatsoever on the outcome of the race? Yes — in fact, that is often the case.

Post position is important to factor in to your handicapping but not more or less so than many other ingredients of the handicapping puzzle. But it is important to note what post positions a horse broke from in its previous races and how it performed from those posts. Perhaps a pattern can be spotted. Perhaps it is more important to see there is no discernable pattern; that a horse can run well from any post.

Could post position be more important for races at sprint distances than distance races? Could the inside post be more favorable at one track than another? Could it matter more on turf than on dirt?

All of these scenarios are quite possible, reinforcing why post position is an important factor in handicapping.

Many horses need to be placed in position earlier during a sprint, so what post position they have becomes more important than if they were running in a longer race. A track that is favoring speed might also favor those runners with inside post positions. And,

THINGS TO KNOW

Depending on a horse's running style (front-runner, from behind, etc.), its post position could help or hinder its chances. Analyze the horse's past performances for clues: Does the horse have enough speed to overcome an outside post? Will he get stuck on the rail from the #1 post? And so on ...

dirt and turf tracks often have very different styles that runners must adjust to.

But who decides which horse breaks from which post? The races take place in the afternoons and evenings, but the entering of horses in a race occurs in the mornings. Entry sheets are filled out by a horse's trainer and placed in the "entry box" in a track's racing office.

Track officials — the racing secretary and his assistants — count up how many horses are entered for each race. Let's return to Gato Del Sol's Derby. Nineteen horses are entered for race. The Churchill Downs officials take nineteen numbered pills and place them together in a bottle for what is called the "pill pull."

They have the nineteen entry sheets, each with the name of a different horse on it. One official pulls an entry sheet out, while another shakes the bottle filled with the pills and pulls one out. The number on the pill is the post position of that particular horse. The process is then repeated eighteen more times.

Cupecoy's Joy, post one; El Baba, number eleven; Gato Del Sol, post eighteen, etc.

It is that simple. And many times, it is that frustrating.

By the time of the post-position draw, a trainer has done everything within his power to get his horse ready for a race — in the case of the Derby, a race he has been pointing toward for months. He has given his horse what he hopes is the proper amount of exercise. He perhaps has nursed his horse along with a slight injury. He has made arrangements for a jockey.

But what if the trainer knows his horse runs better from an inside post position and he draws the outside gate?

Is all that training down the drain? Well, quite frankly, maybe.

Can the horse still win? Yes.

After the draw for the races comprising the 2004 Breeders' Cup, trainer Tom Albertrani had this to say: "Oh great, another inside post."

"Pills" and bottle used for post-position draw.

Albertrani trained the two-year-old filly Balletto, who in her previous four races had broken from post one, two, three, and four. For the Breeders' Cup Juvenile Fillies, she would again break from post one.

Now Balletto had run well, winning three of her first four races. But Albertrani thought she had a greater chance of getting into trouble from the rail.

Handicappers noted how she had won from the inside before and sent her postward as the third choice at 4-1. Balletto ran second to favored Sweet Catomine (who broke from post nine).

A year earlier in the same

Breeders' Cup race, Halfbridled won from the outside post, number fourteen.

Horses can win from any post position, but in handicapping a race, you should take notes regarding how individual horses have done when breaking from different post positions in the starting gate.

By Dan Liebman

8

Medication

Equine medication has been an issue in horse racing for many years, but since the turn of the new century, it has commanded much of the industry's time and energy. Along with the issue of horse health, regulators seek to protect the betting public by attempting to ensure horses don't race on prohibited substances.

It has become accepted practice in racing to treat horses with therapeutic medications, primarily those that reduce inflammation and in turn help horses breathe more easily during competition. Administration of the substances is regulated by state agencies charged with overseeing the sport.

Such regulation includes the testing of blood and urine samples to determine the levels of sub-

stances commonly used in racehorses and to detect the presence of illegal substances. Penalties for horsemen who violate the rules are wide-ranging.

Racetracks usually identify the therapeutic medications used in each horse on race day with marks

in official programs. The therapeutic medications accepted in most racing jurisdictions for use on race day are Salix, an anti-bleeding medication formerly known as Lasix; and aminocaproic acid, which is termed an adjunct bleeder medication. Administration and the amount given to horses are regulated by each state.

Identifying in racetrack programs which horses are racing on which therapeutic medications benefits bettors. For instance, a horse racing on Salix for the first time could improve its performance because it may be able to breathe better or not bleed in the lungs. Perhaps the Salix won't help the horse at all, but many bettors believe "first-time Lasix" may have a positive effect. Though internal, adding a medication is similar to an external equipment change that could help or hinder a horse's ability to race.

Salix is the brand name of furosemide, a diuretic drug used to treat the buildup of fluid in the lungs, as well as heart conditions. In racehorses, it is used to treat exercise-induced pulmonary hem-

---

THINGS TO KNOW

Race-day Medications:

furosemide: anti-bleeding medication; brand name is Salix, though still commonly known by old brand name, **Lasix**. Indicated in track program with **(L)**.

aminocaproic acid: adjunct bleeder medication; brand name is Amicar. Can be used only in certain racing jurisdictions on race day. Indicated in track program with **(A)**.

phenylbutazolidin: a non-steroidal anti-inflammatory (NSAID). Can be used only in certain racing jurisdictions on race day; commonly called "Bute" and indicated in track program with **(B)**.

orrhaging (EIPH), or bleeding in the lungs caused by racing and training.

Though the company that produces furosemide officially changed the name of the medication in 2001 to Salix, the racing industry still mainly uses the old brand name Lasix. It is identified by the letter "L" next to a horse's name in official racetrack programs.

Aminocaproic acid — the most commonly known brand name is Amicar — is a bleeding prevention agent. Several racing states in the Mid-Atlantic region, as well as Ohio, allow use of this medication on race day. Research is ongoing, but officials believe the substance is effective at countering dehydration caused by Salix, thus its classification as an adjunct bleeder medication.

States in which aminocaproic acid is used on race day identify it with an "A" in official racing programs. A horse racing on Salix and Amicar, for instance, will have the letters "LA" next to its name in the program.

Another common therapeutic drug is **phenylbutazolidin**, or "Bute," a highly regulated non-steroidal anti-inflammatory drug (NSAID) used to alleviate pain and swelling. It can be used generally no later than twenty-four hours before a race.

"Bute" is only allowed for race-day use in certain racing jurisdictions and is identified in racing programs with a "B" next to a horse's name.

Therapeutic medications used in racehorses fall under a classification system devised by the Association of Racing Commissioners International (ARCI). There are five classes — Class 5 up to Class 1 — with therapeutics

The (L) next to the horse's name indicates Lasix use.

grouped as Class 4 and Class 5 medications and performance enhancers as Class 2 and Class 1 drugs.

According to ARCI classification guidelines:

• **Class 1** drugs are stimulants and depressants with the highest potential to affect performance. They have no accepted medical use in racehorses and include amphetamines, cocaine, and morphine.

• **Class 2** drugs have a high potential to affect performance, and if they are therapeutic, they have a high potential for abuse. They include alprazolam (Xanax), caffeine, and diazepam (Valium).

• **Class 3** drugs may or may not have accepted medical use in racehorses and have less potential to affect performance. They include bronchodilators such as clenbuterol and antihistamines with sedative properties.

• **Class 4** medications are therapeutic in nature. They include non-steroidal anti-inflammatory drugs, diuretics, anabolic steroids, muscle relaxers, and topical anesthetics.

• **Class 5** medications also are therapeutic in nature and their concentration limits have been established by regulators. They include some local anesthetics and anti-ulcer medications.

Revision of the classification system is just one project being undertaken by the national Racing Medication and Testing Consortium, formed in the wake of an industry-wide Medication Summit in December 2001. The consortium set out to devise guidelines for uniformity in medication use and drug testing for every racing jurisdiction in the United States.

The consortium has suggested grouping all substances into three classes, with appropriate regulations for their use and penalties for their abuse. The panel, which consists of major organizations in the industry, has focused much of its time on uniform race-day medication and research into various substances.

"Race day" can be defined as the twenty-four hours before a race or the morning or afternoon before a race. The consortium thus far has approved only the use of Salix on race day, with uniform administration four hours before a race. It has authorized research into the adjunct bleeder medications currently used in some racing states.

The consortium is advocating uniformity to create a level playing field among racing participants and to protect the wagering public. It also seeks to upgrade drug testing to ensure illegal substances are detected in liquid samples taken from horses.

Drug testing is a rather expensive proposition — some states with year-round, multi-breed racing programs spend millions of dollars a year. Tests generally are performed on a limited number of samples per race.

Blood and urine samples are taken from horses after races and sent to laboratories under contract with regulatory agencies in each state. For high-profile races such as the Kentucky Derby, initial test results can be obtained within forty-eight hours. The typical time period in Kentucky, for instance, is thirteen to fifteen days.

A "positive" — too much of a medication in a horse's system or an illegal drug present — can result in a fine, suspension, and redistribution of purse money after a disqualification.

The national consortium advocates adoption of policies for "prohibited practices" that involve administration of substances believed to enhance performance. The most publicized is a "milkshake," which is a mixture of bicarbonate of soda and a liq-

THE BLOOD-HORSE

Drug tests are performed on a limited number of samples per race.

uid force-fed to a horse through a tube before it competes. A milkshake is said to reduce the buildup of lactic acid in a horse's system, helping prevent or reduce the onset of muscle fatigue and thus enabling the horse to perform more efficiently.

Use of medication in the racehorse is a complex subject that involves regulators, trainers, owners, veterinarians, and chemists. It also directly affects jockeys and their safety. Future courses of action largely hinge on research that ultimately could prove or disprove why certain substances should or shouldn't be used in racehorses.

By Tom LaMarra

9

More Handicapping Factors

In addition to post positions and medication, many other important factors play a part in how you approach handicapping a race. Some of the more common factors many handicappers take into consideration in deciding which horse to play are workout times, change in equipment, and track surfaces. As you progress in your handicapping ability, you'll learn which factors are more important to consider in which races or for certain horses, and you can adjust your handicapping and betting strategies accordingly.

Workouts

Workouts are commonly called "breezes" and are used to get a horse in shape prior to making its first lifetime start or upon returning from a rest. Workouts are also used to keep a horse fit between races. In most cases, a horse will be asked to run right below full speed during a workout. Let's look at the basics of workouts.

Workout Times and Notations

Workouts are measured in furlongs, with an eighth of a mile being equal to one furlong. Workouts are timed in fifths of a second. When a horse steps onto the track to work out, the trainer will notify the official clocker, so the workout is officially recorded. Horses can work out at any distance, but most published workouts begin with a minimum distance of three furlongs.

The official clocker records the name of the horse, the distance, and the time of the workout and may also give some basic information about the workout. Workouts are published daily in racing publications such as the *Daily Racing Form* and are also usually available at a racetrack's customer service center and on the Internet at sites like Equibase.com.

When looking at a published workout (see page 64), you will first see the date (*Feb6*), the track (*Hol*), the distance (*5f*), the track condition (*fst*), the time (*:58*), and a note on how the horse worked, in this case "H" for handily. Below is the explanation for each symbol used to describe a workout:

B — Breezing, the horse was not urged during the workout.

H — Handily, the horse was urged somewhat during the workout.

D — Driving, the horse was asked throughout and usually either shown or struck by the whip during the workout.

G — Gate, the horse worked from the gate (standing still start).

(d) — The horse worked around the dogs, which are orange traffic cones set out on the racetrack away from the rail.

Tr.t — The horse worked on the training track.

"c" — The horse worked in company with other horses (not shown in the *Daily Racing Form*).

Tr — This was a training race, which is essentially a workout when certain horses work together from the gate and the jockeys ride as if it is a real race.

"•" — A bullet next to the workout means the horse worked fastest of the day at that distance.

al, workouts from the gate are slower than non-gate works because of the running start horses get in non-gate works, so take that into consideration when evaluating workout times.

Exercise Rider vs. Jockey and Planning a Workout

A majority of workouts are done with an exercise rider rather than a jockey. Most barns have one or two exercise riders who either gallop or work the horses for that trainer. Of

2 **A. P. Adventure**
White Own: Robert B & Beverly J Lewis
Green, Yellow Hoops And Sleeves, Yellow

B. f. 4 (Jan) FTFFEB03 $425,000
Sire: A.P. Indy (Seattle Slew) $300,000
Dam: Nataliano (Fappiano)
Br: Lazy E Ranch Inc (Ky)
Tr: Dollase Wallace(12 1 2 3 .08) 2004:

DOUGLAS R R (171 34 27 16 .20) 2004: (1297 242 .19)

16Jan05–7SA	fst	1¹⁄₁₆	:23¹ :47	1:10³1:42³	ⒻElEncino-G2	97	7	53½ 62¼	4²	2¹	2hd	
12Dec04–8Hol	fst	1¹⁄₁₆	:23³ :47	1:11 1:41	3↑ⒻBayakoaH-G2	92	1	4³ 42½	5³	41½	3³	
30Apr04–10CD	my	1⅛	:46 1:09⁴	1:36³1:50⁴	ⒻKyOaks-G1	87	8	11¹⁰11¹⁷	9¹³	6¹⁰	69½	
13Mar04–8SA	fst	1¹⁄₁₆	:22⁴ :46²	1:10⁴1:42⁴	ⒻSAOaks-G1	91	5	43½ 32½	52¼	4⁴	3³	
15Feb04–8SA	fst	1	:22³ :46	1:10²1:36²	ⒻLsVrgnes-G1	98	1	6⁶ 5⁴	4⁴	4²	1½	
4Jan04–6SA	fst	1¹⁄₁₆	:23¹ :46⁴	1:11¹1:44¹	ⒻSntYsabl-G3	94	3	6⁶ 4³	3³	3⁴	13½	
30Oct03–1SA	fst	1	:22³ :46²	1:11 1:37⁴	ⒻMd Sp Wt 45k	86	1	55½ 52¼	1¹	1⁴	1⁵	

WORKS: •Feb6 Hol 5f fst :58 H *1/49* • Jan31 Hol 5f fst :59 H *1/40* Jan25 Hol 4f fst :52³ B *23/23* •Jan12 Hol
TRAINER: Dirt(63 .17 $1.07) Routes(83 .22 $1.81) GrdStk(24 .25 $2.07)

Note the workout information at the bottom of a horse's *Daily Racing Form* past performances.

In most cases, each workout is ranked against the workouts of the other horses at the same distance (in this case 1 out of 49 — note the bullet in the above example).

Some notes about the above symbols. Each clocker is different, and what one clocker notes as a breeze (B), another may list as handily (H). While the official clocker strives for accuracy, mistakes do happen. Sometimes a horse is credited with the wrong time or the wrong distance; sometimes his workout is completely missed. Also, a horse working from the gate will start from a still position. In all other workouts, the horse will have a running start before the timing begins. In gener-

course, trainers will also use jockeys to breeze or gallop a horse. The thing to be aware of is that most exercise riders weigh 20 to 30 pounds more than jockeys, and the final time of a workout, to some extent, will be affected by the rider's weight.

Trainers keep a training chart or calendar on each horse. This chart notes the date of the horse's most recent race and potentially the date of the horse's next race. It also notes when the horse has worked out and also may note the horse's next work. When the scheduled workout day comes, the horse will be saddled and taken to the track with either an exercise rider or a jockey. The trainer will give the

FACTORS FOR EVALUATING A WORKOUT

1. Did the rider ask the horse during the work, or did the horse work without being asked?
2. Did the horse work with other horses, or did it work by itself?
3. Was the workout along the rail or did the horse work while wide on the turns?
4. Was the workout right after a track renovation or later, after several horses had galloped or worked over the surface?

Distance	Standard Time
3 furlongs	:36 or faster
4 furlongs	:48 or faster
5 furlongs	1:00 (a minute) or faster

horse's name to the official clocker and also tell the clocker the distance of the workout. Usually, the horse will first warm-up by jogging around the track. When the horse is ready to work out and as it approaches the distance marker of the workout, the rider will ask the horse for some speed. In most cases, the trainer has already told the rider about how fast he wants the horse to work, and the rider will do his best to come close to that time. Some trainers will time each furlong and, via a two-way radio, ask the rider during the workout to pick up speed or slow the horse down.

Of course, the trainer may move up or postpone a workout due to weather.

Each track has a schedule of when horses can work out in the mornings. For example, the track may open for workouts at 5 a.m., close for track maintenance between 7:30 and 8 and then re-open for workouts till 10 a.m. Should a

horse (usually a well-known stakes horse) want to work in the afternoon between races, the trainer will ask the stewards for permission to work the horse either right before live racing starts or between races.

The track is open every morning for workouts, but on rare occasions it may close on a certain day. This may be related to weather or track maintenance.

Evaluating Workouts

Many players will look at workouts for clues on how that horse will run in an upcoming race. One clue is the recorded time. When a horse works out, it is generally accepted that running each furlong in 12 seconds or better is considered "good." The table above shows workout times that are considered "good." However, be aware that many factors go into evaluating workouts, so what appears to

ANNE M. EBERHARDT

A clocker at work.

be a fast or good workout may not be and what appears to be a slow or poor workout may actually be a good workout. Of course, each track and track surface is different, so the table on page 61 may not apply to the track you are playing. You can check the workout tab published in *Daily Racing Form* or posted at customer service centers and compare the workout times of several horses to see what would be a fast or slow work for your track.

It is common for trainers to "blow out" their horse a day or two before a race, sometimes even on the day of the race. These workouts are usually fairly short in distance, such as two or three furlongs and are used to take the edge off a horse or to let a horse stretch its legs before racing. Also, once horses are fit, many may not need a workout between races. The trainer will use long gallops or what are called "two-minute licks," going a mile (once around a mile track) in two minutes to keep the horse in shape.

One last point: While state laws differ, most require a horse to have at least one published workout if that horse has not run within thirty days. On a rare occasion, a horse may have to be scratched if the horse did not meet the minimum required workouts and that horse has not raced for a certain number of days.

Overweights

About a half-hour before the first race, the track announcer will give overweights and changes to the racing fans, and he will give those overweights and changes again prior to each race. In addition, this information is usually posted on the tote board and/or TV monitors throughout the racing day. So, what is an overweight? It is fairly simple to answer that question, but let's take a step back first.

Each race has certain conditions. The purpose of these conditions is to draw horses of similar ability to race against each other. One of those conditions is the amount of weight carried by each horse. This amount of weight may vary for each horse based on the horse's

Many factors go into evaluating workouts.

age, number of wins in the recent past, or the actual claiming price the horse is entered for. Below is an example of a race condition, offering different weights.

In the conditions shown in the box below, if you have a three-year-old filly that has not won a race since July 1 and you enter the horse for $28,000 claiming, the weight assigned will be 115 pounds (starting weight for a three-year-old, 121 pounds, less four pounds as your horse hasn't won since July 1, less another two pounds for entering for $28,000).

The weights of almost all races, excluding stakes and handicaps, are assigned in a way similar to the example below.

Of course, when a horse is entered, the trainer names a jockey to ride. After being entered, the horse is assigned the weight it will have to carry based on the conditions of the race. However, the jockey may not be able to make that assigned weight, and that is where the overweights come from. For example, if the assigned weight for a certain horse is 115 pounds but the rider is 117 pounds, the horse will be two pounds overweight. The clerk of scales weighs each rider before the start of the card, and this weight (rider plus

MATT GOINS

A jockey weighs in after the race.

saddle) is reported to the track stewards, who then notify the track announcer of the overweights.

A couple of notes about overweights: Overweights can change during the racing day. A rider may sit in the hot-box (sweatbox) and lose a pound or two from the time the overweights are announced to the time the race starts. Also, a trainer/owner may switch riders if the original rider cannot make the weight assigned. The trainer/owner may change to a rider that can make the assigned weight. This is rare but does happen on occasion. At smaller tracks, there may be many overweights, or you will notice a dominant rider is always four or five pounds overweight. The connections figure the rider overcomes the extra weight with talent.

Different players place different

> ### RACE CONDITIONS
>
> **Example:**
> Hollywood Park, 5½ furlongs. FClm 32000 (32-28). Purse $25,000. For fillies and mares three years old and upward. Three year olds, 121 lbs; Older, 123 lbs. Non-winners of a race since September 1 allowed 2 lbs. A race since July 1 allowed 4 lbs. Claiming price $32,000, for each $2,000 to $28,000, 1lb.

emphasis on weight and over-weights. Some players keep track of each overweight and may make a change in their selections based on those overweights. Other players ignore overweights.

Equipment

Trainers use many types of equipment to get a horse's best possible performance. When you look at a post parade of any race, you can easily see the equipment. The equipment may be blinkers, a shadow roll, a tongue-tie, front or rear leg wraps, mud calks, and/or a bar shoe. On occasion, the addition of a certain piece of equipment can improve a horse's performance. Other times, the addition of a certain piece of equipment may be a warning all is not right. Let's look at the more common pieces of equipment.

Blinkers — No, these are not related to the turn signal on your car. Blinkers are small plastic cups placed around a horse's eyes to restrict its range of vision. By restricting the range of vision,

> **EQUIPMENT CHECK**
>
> Here's a list of typical racing equip-
> ment in addition to the saddle,
> saddle pad, and bridle:
> - **Shoes:** regular plates, bar shoes,
>   stickers or mud calks
> - **Blinkers and hoods**
> - **Front wraps and rear wraps**
> - **Shadow rolls**
> - **Tongue-ties**
>
> Pay attention to equipment changes
> — shoes and blinkers, especially.

blinkers can help a horse focus on racing rather than on other things, such as other horses, the crowd in the stands, etc. In addition, if a horse has run erratically, blinkers can help it run straight.

Not all blinkers are the same. Blinkers range from what are called "cheater" blinkers, which are blinkers that restrict very little vision to "full cup" blinkers, which may entirely block the vision of one eye. Also, related to blinkers are "screens." Screens are a light wire or cloth mesh and they look very similar to blinkers but protect a horse's eyes from dirt clods other horses kick up during a race.

In all cases, blinker changes are noted at the bottom of your program and in the horse's past performances in the *Daily Racing Form*. "Blinkers On" means the horse is adding blinkers and did not wear them in its previous race. "Blinkers Off" means the horse did run with blinkers in its previous race but is not wearing them for this race.

Handicappers vary in emphasis on the addition or removal of blinkers. In general, the addition of blinkers may help a horse focus more on running and, thus,

Blinkers.

ANNE M. EBERHARDT

improve. The addition of blinkers may also result in a horse's showing more speed early in the race. The removal of blinkers can sometimes help a horse as the lack of blinkers may "wake up" the horse to the other competition in a race. Also, it may help a horse relax early in a race as the horse won't have any fear of not being able to see.

Tongue-Tie — This thin piece of cloth secures the tongue while the horse is running. On occasion, if the tongue is not secured, it may interfere with a horse's breathing. The addition of a tongue-tie is not noted in the program or *Racing Form*, so keeping track of tongue-ties isn't easy. Also, be aware that some trainers will use a certain type of bit that keeps the tongue pressed down while the horse is running. If a horse did have a breathing problem in its previous race, a tongue-tie or a bit change can solve that problem the next time the horse runs.

Shadow Rolls — These are thick bands of fleece placed on the nosebands of horses' bridles. Shadow rolls prevent horses from seeing the ground while they run. Sometimes, a horse will see its shadow or the shadows of other horses and try to jump those shadows. A shadow roll will help prevent this in the horse's next start. Also, some horses will run with their heads high in the air and a shadow roll will help a horse lower its head, allowing the animal to run more smoothly.

Leg Wraps — Trainers can use leg wraps on a horse's front and/or hind legs. Front wraps are either elastic or a combination of cloth and elastic wrapped around a horse's front lower legs and ankles, and they are typically used to pre-

vent nicks and scrapes during a race or workout. Front leg wraps also can help support the legs/ankles of a horse that may have a minor problem with its tendons or ligaments. On a final note, front leg wraps can be placed on a horse or removed from a horse to prevent a claim or attempt to get a horse claimed. For example, if a trainer adds front wraps to a horse, other trainers may be less inclined to claim it as those trainers may

ANNE M. EBERHARDT

Shadow roll.

believe the addition of front wraps may signal a developing physical problem.

Daily Racing Form notes a horse that has previously raced in front wraps or bandages. However, the only way to see if front wraps are a new addition is to observe the horse in the paddock or post parade.

Wraps on the rear legs are typically called "run-downs" and, in most cases, are also used for protection from cuts or scrapes. This protection also helps prevent minor burns from contact with the track surface

Protective wraps and bell boots.

many handicappers will not bet a horse racing in a bar shoe is the mere presence of a bar shoe probably means the trainer has been fighting a minor problem and hasn't been able to prepare a horse for a race properly.

Mud Calks — When the track comes up wet, some trainers will add "mud calks" or "stickers" to the horse's shoes. Mud calks can help a horse get better traction on a wet surface. They are similar to cleats that soccer or football players wear. In most cases, the addition of a mud calk will be noted in the day's overweights and changes or when the field is post parading. Again, mud calks or stickers are used on days when the track is wet, but sometimes a horse may have stickers even if the track is dry.

There are several reasons why a trainer will or won't use mud calks — even on a wet track (if a horse races without mud calks on a day when the track is wet, it is called racing "slick-shod."). The first is adding mud calks costs money, and some trainers may feel the

or from what are called "speedy cuts." Speedy cuts occur when a horse's rear legs contact its front hooves or when its rear legs hit, resulting in gashes.

Shoes — The shoe is a very important piece of equipment for a racehorse. While a horseshoe can be made of any type of metal, a Thoroughbred will race in aluminum shoes, typically called "racing plates," mostly because they are light. On occasion, due to a minor injury or other foot problem, a horse may race in a shoe made of some other material. Also, a shoe may be glued to the foot instead of nailed.

Most shoes are open at the heel, but sometimes a horse will race in what is called a "bar shoe." A bar shoe may cover the entire base of the foot and is used when a horse has a foot problem, most likely a quarter crack. A bar shoe can protect the hoof and prevent the crack from expanding. A horse wearing a bar shoe is usually noted in the track program. The reason

Regular horse shoe.

calks are not worth the added expense. The second reason may be the trainer feels the horse doesn't need mud calks to handle the track. The final reason is some trainers believe that the use of mud calks increases the chances a horse will bruise its foot during a race.

Bar shoes.

ANNE M. EBERHARDT

Gelded — While not directly related to "equipment" (and in this case it could be called a "lack of equipment"), you may hear or read that a horse has been gelded (castrated) since its last start. In some cases you might read this in the program, or you might hear it when overweights and changes are announced. Most male horses are gelded before they first race, but some horses who have decent breeding and high expectations are not gelded as should they become successful on the racetrack they could have a career as a stallion. However, if these horses are not successful on the racetrack, they may be gelded to try and improve their performance. Again, a horse

gelded between starts is usually noted in the program or when overweights and changes are announced. Knowing a horse has been recently gelded is important: Gelding may lead to an improvement on the racetrack, because the horse, in most cases, will be easier to handle and train.   *By John Lindley*

Track Surface

Handicapping horse races goes well beyond assessing the chances of horses based strictly on past performances. There are many other factors, not the least of which are the surfaces on which horses compete.

FUN HANDICAPPING "METHODS"

So, you just want to bet and have fun and not worry about the myriad of information it takes to handicap a race successfully? Here are few fun "methods" that may not help you cash a ticket; however, you'll have a good time trying. But as with any visit to the track, be sure to watch your spending.

Your birthday, anniversary, mom's birthday, etc.: Bet the horse if your birthday (or anniversary, etc.) matches the horse's birth date.

Grey horses: They stand out amidst all those bays, so why not bet on one?

Cutest jockey: Female patrons mainly use this approach. You can hope said jockey is also the track's leading rider.

Dead and exiled sires: If the horse's sire has recently died or been exported, it's a sure sign the horse will win.

Name hunch: If a horse's name reminds you in any way of a relative, friend, favorite song, etc., etc., give it a try.

Racing in North America is predominantly contested on the dirt, though grass racing — commonly called turf racing — continues to gain in popularity and frequency. In other parts of the world, such as Australia, Great Britain, and Ireland, the opposite is true — most races are held on the turf.

Though dirt racing is standard in the United States, actually very little about it is standard. Weather conditions and climate play major roles in the condition of a racing surface, as does the composition of the surface. In addition, not all racetracks

A sloppy track.

are the same circumference.

The condition of a racing surface for each race is recorded in past performances by the official chart-callers. Here's a list of surface conditions for dirt tracks:

Fast: The term seems to indicate speed, but generally it means a surface is dry. Still, horses usually record the fastest times on fast tracks.

Wet-fast: The surface is fast but has some moisture on top, usually from rain. The water, however, hasn't seeped in, so horses have a tendency to skip over the surface.

Good: The surface is a shade duller than fast. The surface is drying out but contains some moisture.

Muddy: The word describes it perfectly. The surface is wet and somewhat deep.

Sloppy: The surface is soaked, with water lying on top.

Frozen: Moisture in the track is frozen because of cold temperatures. The surface may look dry and fast and often produces quick times because of its hardness.

Heavy and **Slow:** These two terms are hardly used anymore, but they speak for themselves. Because of conditions, the surface is somewhat tiring and produces abnormally slow times.

For turf racing, conditions are similar:

Firm: This is similar to fast on the dirt. The course is dry but has some give to it.

Good: The course retains some moisture.

Soft: The course is fairly wet.

Yielding: The course is very wet and times are rather slow.

Hard: This term is rarely used, but it means the course is extremely dry and has very little give.

For handicapping purposes, some horses like a dry surface, while others like a wet one. In the old days, *Daily Racing Form* would identify horses that preferred wet tracks with "mud marks" in their past performances. Now, the *Form* and track programs list the number of starts on a wet track as well as first-, second-, and third-place finishes. Similar information is available for turf racing.

A horse's record on "off" tracks

ANNE M. EBERHARDT

(non-fast tracks) is to be used as a guide. Horses throw in clunkers no matter the track condition, and only those with high win or in-the-money percentages on wet tracks, or those that always display form reversals on wet tracks, are considered true "mudders."

Though consistency of performance is an important ingredient, so is consistency of the track surface. There are times when certain running styles — up close early or come from behind, for example — have a definite edge. The situation could be triggered by everything from track condition to the way the dirt is scraped or harrowed. Often you may hear that the rail is "deep" in regards to a muddy surface, and bettors might avoid horses with inside post positions who are likely to get stuck on the rail because the "deeper" path along the rail supposedly is slower.

Such track biases aren't detailed in past-performance information. Therefore, watching as many races as possible is helpful. Only then can a handicapper assess whether a horse's chances were severely compromised because it didn't have the right running style or because it raced on an unfavorable part of the surface on a given day.

Be mindful that track conditions can change not only day-to-day but race-to-race. Heavy rain that renders a track sloppy in the middle of a program, or a surface that begins thawing out midway through a program, can create, shift, or eliminate biases.

ANNE M. EBERHARDT

Racing on firm turf.

One of the best examples came on a Saturday afternoon one winter at Turfway Park, where the racing surface is subject to freeze-thaw conditions. For the first six races, the surface favored speed. But as a heavy snow fell and moisture worked its way into the surface, off-the-pace runners developed an edge. By the end of the program, front-runners had no shot.

Another piece of information not included in past performances is the circumference of a racetrack, which varies from a half-mile at some county fairs to one and a half miles at Belmont Park in New York. The majority of Thoroughbred dirt tracks are one mile in circumference, and most turf courses are seven-eighths of a mile because they are positioned inside the dirt tracks.

Tracks less than one mile in circumference are called "bull rings." Such facilities used to be associated with lower-quality racing, but gaming-fueled purse increases have attracted quality horses to such "bull rings" as Charles Town Races & Slots in West Virginia and Delta

Downs Racetrack & Casino in Louisiana, for instance.

Handicapping at such tracks requires more consideration for post positions because the turns are tighter and the homestretches shorter. Horses can be carried very wide and lose momentum. It's also important to note that a standard six-furlong event on a one-mile track is raced around one turn, while the same distance on a five-eighths-mile or three-quarter-mile track (six furlongs) requires a horse to negotiate two turns. The biggest impact of an additional turn or two is slower fractional and final times for various distances. Thus, if a horse records a six-furlong time of 1:12 on a two-turn track, it should receive additional consideration when it competes against horses timed in 1:12 going one turn.

By Tom LaMarra

10

Pedigree Handicapping

As racing fans file through the turnstiles, most are armed with a pocket full of cash, a *Racing Form*, a program, and a theory of how to make money at the betting windows. Many factors influence a betting decision, including something as seemingly insignificant as a horse's bloodline. Pedigree is a viable component of handicapping for those who are astute enough to recognize it. And scenarios like this one play out every day at every track across the country:

The sixth race on the card, a one and one-sixteenth-mile maiden special weight on the turf, has a field of ten. One entry, a compact muscular chestnut colt has attracted the eye of the betting public. His past performances are promising; his workouts, bullets. What's not to like? Heading into the final furlongs, he looks like money in the bank. But as his stride shortens, he is passed by a large, coarse dark bay son of a former turf star. His previous races, all contested at less than seven furlongs on dirt, had been even at best. But it is a new day, a new distance, a new surface. As this 20-1 shot comes bounding down the grassy stretch, ears pricked and looking for some competition, bettors scratch their heads in amazement, hoping somehow the number on the ticket would miraculously change or the mutuel clerk made a mistake. Wondering how this horse could have won so easily, they turn again to their *Racing Forms*. With the clarity of hindsight, they discover the answer had been there all along, in black and white. Just not in the usual place. For this particular race, the winning key lay not in the precise

world of Beyer and Ragozin figures or of times measured in hundredths of seconds or of who had beaten whom by how many lengths. Rather, the answer lay in the seemingly insignificant, and often overlooked, names that detail the lineage of the horses, the pedigree.

The names on the pedigree line are simple manifestations of a much more complex world of DNA and RNA, fast-twitch and slow-twitch muscle fibers, and mitochondrial contribution. These are the genetic components of performance.

Think of it this way: Learning to read a pedigree is a kind of CliffsNotes study course for the handicapping test, given on any day at your local racetrack. Apples don't fall far from their trees, and so it is with most horses. You would not expect a youngster with

THINGS TO KNOW

Internet resources for pedigrees:

www.bloodhorse.com
www.chef-de-race.com
www.pedigreequery.com

Pedigrees 101

A pedigree is a horse's family tree. The following example is Smarty Jones' four-generation pedigree (his parents are considered the first generation).

Elusive Quality, 1993 [1] [9]	**Gone West, 1984** [5]	Mr. Prospector [7]	Raise a Native / Gold Digger [8]
		Secrettame	Secretariat / Tamerett
	Touch of Greatness, 1986 [6]	Hero's Honor	Northern Dancer / Glowing Tribute
		Ivory Wand	Sir Ivor / Natashka
SMARTY JONES / **I'll Get Along, 1992** [2]	**Smile, 1982** [3]	In Reality	Intentionally / My Dear Girl
		Sunny Smile	Boldnesian / Sunny Sal
	Dont Worry Bout Me, 1983 [4]	Foolish Pleasure	What a Pleasure / Fool-Me-Not
		Stolen Base	Herbager / Bases Full

[1]	Sire (father)	[6]	Paternal granddam
[2]	Dam (mother)	[7]	Great-grandparents
[3]	Broodmare sire or damsire	[8]	Great-great-grandparents
[4]	Second dam or granddam	[9]	Year of birth
[5]	Paternal grandsire		

In the *Daily Racing Form*, pedigrees appear this way:

Sire: Elusive Quality (Gone West)
Dam: I'll Get Along (Smile)

In most racetrack programs, pedigrees appear in a pedigree line:

SMARTY JONES
Ch.c.3, Elusive Quality—I'll Get Along by Smile

a stamina-laden pedigree to win at four furlongs; conversely, you would not put much faith in, or much money on, a horse whose parents were best at six furlongs to win a nine-furlong race around two turns.

The first step, therefore, is to learn to read a pedigree line. Usually three names make up a pedigree line. First is the sire (father) of the horse. Next is the dam (mother), followed by the name of the broodmare sire or damsire (see example opposite. These are immediate genetic contributors for the horses listed in the entries. Each parent donates half the genetic material of the offspring, and the biographies of these horses provide valuable insight into the qualities the offspring has inherited. For example, one of the entries is a son of classic-winning A.P. Indy out of a mare by Nijinsky II (a winner of the English Triple Crown), both noted sources of class and stamina, and the race is over a route of ground. These names and the information they represent indicate this is indeed a horse suited for the task at hand. Such an entry would become an even more attractive betting proposition by going off as an overlay, where the odds are far greater than the horse's chances of winning. A trip to the paddock reveals a tall, rangy horse with a well-developed shoulder, the type of build more suited to distance races. That seals the deal. This is a prime opportunity to cash a winning ticket. Unfortunately, there is no such thing as a sure thing, but you can maximize the potential of winning through careful examination and evaluation of all kinds of data, pedigree included.

Using pedigrees to handicap races is not something done casually. Oh, occasionally, you might have that beginner's luck and pick a horse that wins a race because you have heard of the sire or of the dam. However, that is not a method that will work over the course of your betting life. The more you follow horse racing as a sport and not just as a vehicle for betting, the better you will be at using pedigrees to handicap races because you will become familiar with which sires produce runners with early speed, which sires produce runners with stamina, and which sires produce runners with a proclivity for the turf or off-tracks. This knowledge forms your own database from which you can extract necessary bits and bytes on any given race day.

However, there's also prior preparation. You know, that thing that prevents poor performance. When you were in school, it was called homework and studying. The same process holds true for a day at the track. If you are interested in winning money at the races and bragging rights for the exacta you played that paid more than $300, it's worth putting in some time "poring over the books." Start by looking over the races carded for the next day. Some races lend themselves to handicapping better than others; some races you might want to avoid altogether. This is especially important if you are using pedigrees as a tool for handicapping a race. It's not a method for every race. Look for maiden races, especially those for two-year-olds. Also, look for races in which horses are asked to do something for the first time. Perhaps it's the first time at a distance or the first time on the turf. Perhaps the race is on a track that is anything less than fast or it's a race that has been taken off the turf. Races like these lend themselves to letting pedigree guide your decisions.

Now the question becomes how a relative novice to horse racing can find this information quickly enough. A good starting place is the Internet. Using a search engine like Google, for example, you can find some information about most things. By putting in key words and hitting search, knowledge flies to the screen with a click of the mouse.

In addition to search engines, there are many Web sites that contain information that will stand you in good stead. If you are interested in sires, Web sites such as bloodhorse.com contain current sire lists, which can be accessed for free. Trade publications, such as *The Blood-Horse*, also publish leading sires lists in each issue. These lists are often much more helpful as they are more specific and contain more detailed information. For example, you may be able to find the leading sires of two-year-olds, the leading turf sires, and even the leading broodmare sires.

An important Web site for finding information as to what kind of performers many of the first-rate sires were is chef-de-race.com. Here you can find grouped by aptitude those sires that have been chosen the most outstanding influences on pedigrees. They are divided into five groups: brilliant, intermediate, classic, solid, and professional. Sires in the brilliant and intermediate ranges are more speed-oriented

while sires in the solid and professional categories are more stamina-oriented. Using these sires to help decipher pedigrees can prove invaluable.

While information on sires is relatively easy to find, finding out about the dam may prove to be more difficult. If the dam is a well-known mare, an Internet search engine may prove fruitful. Did the dam win stakes? At what distance? Has she produced any stakes winners? What kinds of races did they win? However, many mares bloom unnoticed, being unraced or just winners. Here you might need some more information. A more extensive pedigree, at least three-generation, will give information about the female family. Look at the second and third dams. Did they win stakes? Have they produced stakes winners and at what distance, surface, etc.? A good Web site for looking at a five-cross pedigree is pedigreequery.com. Here you can look at a five-cross pedigree for free. Additional information is available but a membership is required.

If you can't find any information about the mare, you can always look at the broodmare sire for some indication. Approach the broodmare sire as you would the sire. First examine broodmare sire lists, and move on from there.

Many other sources are available to help you integrate pedigrees into your handicapping methods. Among these are Steven A. Roman's *Dosage: Pedigree and Performance*, Lauren Stich's *Pedigree Handicapping*, and Mike Helm's *Exploring Pedigree*.

By Tom Hall

11

Speed Figures

Speed figures, available to handicappers through many avenues, offer bettors the opportunity to compare horses in a field through a system devised by professionals.

These professionals come up with a number for a horse's effort that can apply from track to track and day to day, so the same figure at Belmont or Santa Anita on a given day should mean the same thing as a figure earned at Delaware Park or Turf Paradise on another day.

Speed figures are most helpful in claiming races, which make up approximately 66 percent of all racing programs, giving some insight into a horse's true ability, not just its claiming value.

Speed figures exploded onto the Thoroughbred-betting scene in the 1980s and early 1990s. The wide availability of these figures changed the landscape of handicapping in North America, taking away a huge edge from the most sophisticated bettors. Speed figures now appear in most track programs and the *Daily Racing Form*, and also can be purchased directly from some distributors for a fee.

Beyer speed figures, the Thoro-Graph figures, and the Ragozin numbers are the most recognized in the game. The Beyer speed figures, developed by Andy Beyer, a sportswriter with *The Washington Post*, rise with the better efforts, so the higher the number the better, while the Thoro-Graph and Ragozin numbers, or "sheets," go the opposite way — the lower the number the better.

Rarely do handicappers use more than one type of speed figure, usually relying on the one they are most familiar with.

Beyer speed figures are the most popular and most widely available, as they are used in the *Daily Racing Form* past performances. A poor effort can earn Beyer numbers in the 40-50 range, and the best of efforts can score in the 120 area. For example, Horse of the Year Ghostzapper, winner of the 2004

Ghostzapper posted a record Beyer figure in 2004.

ALEXANDER BARKOFF

Track bias and the trouble a horse encounters are not included in the calculation of most speed figures.

Breeders' Cup Classic, earned a 124 Beyer speed figure that afternoon at Lone Star Park. He also posted the highest two-turn Beyer speed figure in 2004 with a 128 for his Philip Iselin Breeders' Cup Handicap victory. In fact, it was the highest Beyer figure recorded in the past nine years. Low-level claimers will earn Beyer numbers in the mid-60s range.

Speed figures are not calculated until after each day's card of racing because the biggest factor in their determination is how fast or slow a track played throughout the day at a particular track. In other words, the key to an accurate speed figure is determining how the speed of the surface affected the final times on any given day. That is done by calculating a variant.

A variant is derived for the day after the final times of each race are compared against a historical average, which is obtained by averag-

ing actual final times of each class level in the past and is commonly called a "par."

While Beyer figures are adjusted for the speed of the surface and lengths beaten (if any), they don't consider the pace of the race, the track bias (if there is one), and any trouble a horse might have encountered. The Thoro-Graph and Ragozin numbers don't incorporate track biases or troubled trips into their figures either, however, Thoro-Graph does note track biases on its sheets. Ragozin and Thoro-Graph sheets do incorporate speed of the surface, weight carried, lengths beaten (if any), wind, and ground loss, such as when a horse races wide, into their figures and include notations next to a figure for bad trips. For example, if a horse breaks slowly, then has to check, is stuck on the rail, and so on, that is not included in the figure but will be noted alongside.

The most important thing to remember when using speed figures is to recognize they only tell you what a particular horse did — not what it is going to do. If a horse earned a super-high Beyer number in its previous race or an extremely low one, you should consider what factors came into play. The number is not indicative of how the horse will run next time out, as the horse will be facing a totally different scenario.

However, some hard-and-fast criteria have been proven over time. Certain class levels of horses run similar numbers over certain tracks. The *Daily Racing Form* periodically publishes three-year averages, broken down by claiming, maiden, allowance, and stakes levels at the major tracks. If you are looking to handicap claiming races, for example, a starting point is knowing what the average figure is for that level and distance. If a horse has consistently run near the average for a particular level, or even above that figure, he's a contender worthy of another look. If he hasn't, and certain pace scenarios don't appear to play in his favor on this day, then pass. In a good-sized field of horses, if you can

whittle the cast to three or four playable contenders, then you're in business to break down other important handicapping variables, such as recent work patterns, post position, and certain running styles before you wager.

While interpretation of speed figures is the key, there are certain scenarios to look for and certain traps to avoid. One of the easiest traps to fall into is placing too much emphasis on the "last race figure." If a horse earned an all-time best number in its previous start, especially after a layoff, then consider looking elsewhere. Most horses, with the exception of the upper-echelon horses, can rarely duplicate or surpass a career-best number in back-to-back starts.

One exception to this rule is the "Omni fig" horse — a scenario defined by Andy Beyer. In the

Beyer speed figures in the *Form*.

Equibase speed figures in track program.

lower-level claiming races, every so often you'll run across a horse that earned a figure in its previous race that is higher than any number ever earned by the other horses in the field. This scenario happens rarely, but when it does, the horse has a tremendous class edge and usually wins ... and wins big. His past exploits haven't gone unnoticed, however, as this horse usually is at a price substantially less than 2-1.

If a horse drops substantially off a high-end figure in its next start, that's what is generally called a "bounce." This happens a large percentage of the time in a horse's second start off a layoff. Taking it a step further, on a good number of occasions, a horse will "bounce back" in its third start off the rest with a much-improved effort off its second start.

Another caveat in interpreting speed figures comes in turf races, especially turf route races. In American racing there aren't the solid numbers of turf races run annually at one track to get a large enough sample to come up with true "pars" and "variants." Additionally, the pace scenarios and trouble encountered in turf races make it difficult to use speed figures with any conviction. The dynamic in turf races around two turns is unique, and a better way to attack the race is from the class angle, studying the pace and final closing times of the horses to separate the contenders from the pretenders.

By Evan Hammonds

Trip Handicapping

Trip handicapping requires being a true student of the game — nothing more, nothing less. Its key component is a non-biased analysis of a race after it has been run to gain insight into how a future race might unfold. It takes time and effort … but it's worth it.

If you've backed a specific horse, it's easy to follow that runner in the race and see any trouble it may have encountered during its trip. The problem is you're focused on just that one horse and not the whole race. Trip handicapping comes into play after the event, with an in-depth study of not only that horse but the other horses in the race. Replays are readily available after the race has been run, and most tracks have areas where you can watch replays, including the all-important head-on view.

The head-on replay will help show trouble areas more clearly,

and you can take special note of a horse's action. You can also observe if a horse runs in a straight line, lugs in, or drifts out, suggesting it was tired from its efforts or unfit for the task.

When reviewing the replay, take time to watch more than one horse and take notes of any trouble that might have occurred. And then, most importantly, ask yourself as many questions as possible. How did certain horses act in the gate, and how did they break? Was the horse hindered by an inside or outside post? Did the horse encounter traffic on the turn or have to go

Race replays are invaluable for good trip handicapping.

83

A typical "cavalry charge" finish in a turf race.

extremely wide around the turns? When asked to "make its move," did the horse encounter difficulty at any point? Those are the most obvious questions. Try to ask yourself many more.

There are dozens of questions to ask about a certain "trip." Circumstances of the race also play an important factor in trip handicapping. Was the pace too brisk? Was an individual runner alone on the lead? How did the fractions compare to those in other races run that day?

Trip handicapping is also "pace handicapping." Pace handicapping is analyzing a race according to which horse or horses you think will dictate the early tempo. If you think a horse can get an easy early lead, it may be able to wire the field. If there seems to be plenty of pace in a race, then a late-running horse might be able to close and win.

All these observations need to be documented and kept for future races. In essence, note what a horse did and how. By looking back, you can look to future efforts. What's the best way to do this? Don't rely on memory alone, so if you keep programs, make notations there. If not, keep a notebook. An even better idea might be to record notes on the computer, using a spreadsheet program that you can sort by horses' name, track, date, and so on.

But be aware that past efforts may or may not come into play in today's race. You still need to analyze each scenario and determine if the horse you are considering will get a better "trip" this time around and how its running style compares to the other horses' styles.

Several things should be kept in mind. Any trouble you spot won't go unnoticed by others; therefore, horses that recently had trouble most likely will be overbet next time out by other "trip handicappers," thereby forcing the odds down.

Some horses repeatedly have "tough" trips, and they don't have to be racing against a large field to find trouble. A horse can get blocked or checked just as easily in a five-horse field as in a twelve-horse field. It might be that the horse truly does have bad luck with encountering traffic trouble, but the horse could also just not be athletic enough to overcome the trouble, so you would probably want to use caution when betting a runner like this.

Finding a horse that experiences trouble in turf races is also easy but for a different reason. Most horses that encounter some sort of "trouble" in a turf race do so because of the narrower turf course layouts and sharper turns at North American tracks, where nearly all of the turf courses are on the inside of the dirt track. Also, the pace of turf races is different than it is in dirt races, with a stronger emphasis on the final furlongs as opposed to the first furlongs of a dirt race. A large percentage of turf races results in a cavalry charge in the stretch, where trouble spots abound. Again, these "troubled" horses will be overbet in their following race regardless of how that race shapes up.

Another key element of trip handicapping is "track bias,"

> ### TRIP TIPS
>
> When trip handicapping, remember these key points:
> - Ask as many questions as possible about a race.
> - Keep notes about each horse for future reference.
> - Compare the running styles of the horses in a field.
> - Horses coming off a "troubled" trip will usually be overbet.
> - True track biases can be difficult to determine.

which is harder to determine. A track bias occurs when a certain track surface, or part of the surface area, gives a runner a distinct advantage. The most common bias is the "speed bias" or "golden rail," where the inside part of the track is playing faster than other parts of the track.

It's hard to determine when a track bias exists, but it usually takes place after wet weather when the track surface changes from very wet to drying out.

Usually after the first two or three races on a card, some wiseguy horseplayer will loudly pronounce, "There's a speed bias," or "The rail is golden today." Remember, it's extremely difficult to pick up on a certain track bias early on the card. Review the past performances and replays of the

Bred in Kentucky by Fletcher Gray & Carolyn Gray (May 25, 1998)

		Jockey: **R. R. Douglas** (265-59-48-35)							
		Trainer: **Bernard S. Flint** (20-3-3-2)							
123		Life:	12	5	2	1	$283,313	Dist: 6 3 1 0	$140,210
		2001:	6	2	2	1	$206,304	Wet: 2 0 0 0	$810
		2000:	5	3	0	0	$76,199	Turf: 0 0 0 0	$0

114	fL	3.10	94	90 DrmSprme 4$\frac{3}{4}$,HdnAsts 3$\frac{1}{2}$,SgrNSpce nk	in tight st, no match
115	fL	2.90	93	91 Trp $\frac{1}{2}$,HdenAsets $\frac{3}{4}$,RseofZolem 5$\frac{3}{4}$	exchanged bumps start
121	fL	*.50	77	71 ComeSeptember $\frac{3}{4}$,CapitolView 1$\frac{3}{4}$,FacciaBella 1	gave way
117	fL	*1.10	87	91 MrchMagic 1$\frac{1}{2}$,PnyBlues $\frac{3}{4}$,HdenAsets 1$\frac{1}{4}$	off rail, weakened

h 1/20   Bred in Kentucky by Gainesway Thoroughbreds Limited (April 21, 1997)

Jockey: **Robby Albarado** (121-37-17-18)	
Trainer: **Robert E. Holthus** (25-3-0-3)	

Comments such as "in tight" and "exchanged bumps" indicate troubled trips.

early races. Perhaps it's merely a matter of a front-runner being left alone on the lead and easily winning. Judging a track bias is highly subjective.

If a pronounced bias exists, taking advantage of it is extremely difficult. By the end of the day, if there is a pronounced rail bias, the jockeys have picked up on it and they'll be hustling their mounts out early to try to get to the lead and the rail. These races, too, require detailed note taking and later evaluation.

You can't truly recognize a track bias on a given day until perhaps two or three weeks later when horses coming out of those events race again. The best way to take advantage of a track bias is to observe those horses that were either helped or hindered and assess how they performed in their next starts. Did a horse that had a "golden rail trip" last time run a similar race next time out, or did he fade in the stretch over a non-biased surface? Was a closer able to make up more ground this time than last time out? If a true bias was detected, then other horses coming out of those previous races should be followed. There are ways to take advantage of track biases, but rarely can you do it on a given day. It's best to observe, take notes, and wait for certain runners to resurface down the road.

By Evan Hammonds

Turfway Park - March 4, 2005 - Race 10
Allowance — For Thoroughbred Three Year Old Fillies (NW1X) Six and One-Half Furlongs on the Dirt

Purse $25,400. Includes $10,000 (Kentucky Thoroughbred Development Fund)
Value of race $25,400. 1st $15,740; 2nd $5,080; 3rd $2,540; 4th $1,270; 5th $462; 6th $308.

Horse	A	Wgt	M/E	Odds	PP	SP	1/4	1/2	Str	Fin	Jockey
She's That Cat	3	119	L	3.20	3	5	$2^{2\frac{1}{2}}$	2^1	1^1	1^2	Mojica, O.
Salty Beach	3	111	L	6.60	5	3	6	5^1	4^6	$2^{1\frac{1}{2}}$	Molina Jr., J.
Independent Cat	3	116	L	1.30*	4	1	$1^\frac{1}{2}$	1^{hd}	2^3	3^{nk}	Sarvis, D.
Charlie My Boy	3	116	L bf	4.40	2	4	4^4	3^8	$3^{2\frac{1}{2}}$	4^9	Prescott, R.
Bubble N Squeak	3	122	L	3.90	6	2	3^1	$4^\frac{1}{2}$	5^2	$5^{2\frac{1}{2}}$	Ouzts, P.
Moneybackguarantee	3	116	L b	26.80	1	6	5^3	6	6	6	Patin, B.

Off Time: 9:30　　Time Of Race: :22.84　　:46.09　　1:11.33　　1:18.25
Start: Good for all　　Track: Fast
Equipment: b for blinkers, f for front wraps

Pgm	Horse	Win	Place	Show
5	She's That Cat	$8.40	$4.20	$3.00
7	Salty Beach		5.40	3.40
6	Independent Cat			2.60

Wager	Type	Winning Numbers	Payoff
$2	Exacta	5-7	$44.00
$2	Supertecta	5-7-6-4	$268.60
$2	Trifecta	5-7-6	$123.20

Winner: She's That Cat, b f, by American Chance—Palmbeachpussycat, by Storm Cat (Trained by Larry W. Demeritte)
Bred by Walter B. Mills in KY

Scratched: Judy's Gem, Upshot

SHE'S THAT CAT pressed the pace off the inside, took over in midstretch and slowly increased her advantage. SALTY BEACH outrun early, raced four wide on the turn and finished full of run on the outside. INDEPENDENT CAT set a pressured pace along the inside and tired late. CHARLIE MY BOY within striking distance, raced three wide on the turn and lacked a late bid. BUBBLE N SQUEAK behind the leaders, raced in the four path on the turn and gave way in the drive. MONEYBACKGUARANTEE was no factor.

© EQUIBASE CO.

---

the meet's leading jockey Dean Sarvis is named to ride her again for the leading trainer, Greg Foley. (Look for a track's leading jockey and trainer stats in the *Form* or track program.)

The #7, **Salty Beach** (6-1; 7-1), is a dedicated come-from-behind runner that finished behind Judy's Gem in her last start. She has been unable to clear this condition in four attempts but likes this distance and is another that could be in the right spot at the right time should a speed duel develop early.

The #8, **Bubble N Squeak** (5-1; 4-1), hasn't raced since last October for trainer Ken McPeek, who has his better stock in Florida for the winter. This filly has been working out at Palm Meadows Training Center in South Florida and ships north for easier pickings. She takes a considerable drop in class, having competed in a grade III stakes two starts back in Illinois. This is another runner with early speed but she drew the outside post, which means she could be hung wide should others to her inside go for the early lead.

Using what you've learned in this guide, what other factors would you consider? Who would you pick and what kind of bet(s) would you make? Check out the race result to see how you would have fared.

Myth Busters
Misconceptions of wagering

When you are at the races, you will hear all sorts of phrases from different people. Many of these phrases are repeated so often they are accepted as fact by some players. In most cases, a little truth lies behind each myth. However, let's take a look at some of these myths or misconceptions and discuss the real truth behind them.

1. "You can beat a race, but you can't beat the races."

This is probably the oldest and most-often quoted phrase. The implication of this phrase is that while you can get lucky and make money on an individual race, the more times you go to the track and the more races you play, the better chance you will lose. There is a little truth behind this phrase, because for the most part a majority of people who play the races do lose money. The average takeout on straight wagers is 18 percent; the average takeout on exotic wagers is 22 percent. This leaves a blended takeout of 20 percent, which means for every dollar bet on horse racing, 80 cents is returned to the public. The math means most people must lose as each dollar wagered is chasing only 80 cents in payoffs.

However, the real truth is pretty much the opposite. The phrase should say, "You can't beat a race, but you can beat the races." The nature of horse race betting is that it is a competition among bettors. The betting public determines the odds of each horse by the amount of money bet on each horse. Those odds may or may not be an accu-

rate representation of a horse's true odds. In other words, the public is sometimes wrong in assessing the true chances of each horse. If you are able to find situations in which the public is wrong in the betting because you are a better handicapper and decision-maker, you can win. The second reason that phrase is backward is you can't always know what might happen in any one race. There are many ways for the best horse to be beaten, such as a troubled trip, a minor injury, bad tactics by the rider, etc. You may be right about a race but not cash a ticket because of one of these events. However, hopefully, over time the bad luck is evened out with the good luck, and betting on the races can be profitable.

2. "They want certain horses, such as favorites, to win." (with "they" referring to racetrack management)

This one is also a myth because racetracks don't have a vested interest in the outcome of any race. In other words, the racetrack gets the same amount of money from the total handle on a race whether any particular horse — such as the favorite — wins, runs second, or finishes out of the top three. The

A racetrack gets the same amount of money from a race's handle regardless of where the favorite finishes.

amount of money is a certain percentage of the takeout and is established by law. So this presumption is a myth, but there is partial truth to the myth.

If you asked what would be a perfect day regarding results, track management would prefer a day during which mostly favorites won with a few longshots mixed in. If a longshot won every race, as the day progressed the general public would have less and less money to wager, as the winning bettors would be the few who had those longshots. The effect of this is to leave most players broke and betting less, thus decreasing the amount of money a racetrack gets from that handle.

If favorites win every race, more people continue to have money to bet as the day progresses, and the total handle may rise. The disadvantage of this is that low payoffs turn players off, and they may look to other tracks. Finally, if the track offers a pick six wager, carryovers generate excitement and large car-ryovers generate higher handles and bigger crowds, so having a couple of days with longshots can help the track.

As a side note, racetracks don't have any control over disqualifications or steward's decisions. Track stewards are not employees of the racetrack; they are employees of the state racing commission and are independent of racetracks.

Again, the point is that, with a few exceptions, racetracks have no vested interest in which horse wins any individual race.

3. "Scared money never wins."

This phrase implies that if you are betting with money that should be used for other things (commonly called "scared money"), such as your rent or mortgage money or money for food, you will not win. It suggests that you won't win because the added pressure of playing with money you can't afford to lose will lead you to make wrong decisions.

Of course, this phrase implies if

you are betting with money you can afford to lose, you will be better off as the pressure of needing to win is removed. While I don't suggest betting the rent money on races, I also believe the truth lies somewhere in-between. I have noticed that people who have all the money they need — millionaires, very successful business people, people who are in the "inheritance business," or lottery winners, etc. — come to the races and because money means nothing to them, they lose and tend to lose a lot. They don't realize the amount of work and discipline needed to win at the races. At the same time, they tend to bet every race and they often bet several horses in each race. They are just looking for action, as neither winning nor losing would affect anything in their life.

Contrast these bettors with those who can't afford to lose. This type of bettor will have the desire to win at the races as losing does "cost"

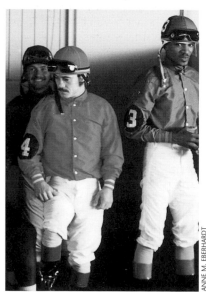

Jockeys are not always objective about their horse's chances.

something and may spend the time trying to be successful at the track and make good handicapping and betting decisions. While trying to make a living as a professional bettor isn't in the cards for a large majority of racing fans, some work and discipline can lead to a profitable hobby.

4. "Watch the tote board for the smart money" — and the related phrase mentioned after a race **"they knew the horse was going to win."**

These phrases imply that the trainers, owners, and jockeys know if their horses are going to win and by seeing which horse gets bet late, you can jump on board the winning horse. The biggest problem with this idea is that owners, trainers, and jockeys don't know if their horses are going to win. Don't get me wrong; trainers, jockeys, and owners sometimes do possess some information on their horse that would be beneficial to know. However, the biggest reason this idea is a myth is that those trainers, jockeys, and owners are, in most cases, not objective. They are not looking at the race from a handicapping perspective. In other words, they tend to see only their horse and may not know, for example, that another horse didn't care for the wet track in his last race, bled the race before, and had a tough trip two races back. In addition, they have no control over what happens after the gates open.

Watching the tote board for late money or listening to tips from owners, trainers, or jockeys may work once or twice, but you will be better off over the long run by sticking with your opinion because

Don't dismiss betting a favorite if you feel the odds warrant it.

you are better able to evaluate each horse's chances objectively. In fact, if an owner came up to me and hinted he had information and asked if I would like to hear it, I would say, "I will give you $20 if you don't tell me."

5. "You must bet overlays to win" or a related, similar phrase **"you can't win betting the favorite."**

Well the first part of this hypothesis is true; however the second part is a myth. The problem with the first part is defining what constitutes an overlay. There are a lot of misconceptions when it comes to determining if a horse is an underlay or an overlay in the betting. For example, let's say you encounter a race in which a horse is 3-5 and the guy next to you says, "I wouldn't bet any horse at 3-5." He may be implying that any horse that goes off at odds of 3-5 is overbet, thus an underlay. However, if you feel a horse such as this has a better than 60 percent chance of winning, 3-5 is actually an overlay

based on that assumption. In other words a heavily bet horse sometimes is an overlay, and a 20-1 shot sometimes is an underlay, based on your belief of that horse's chances.

Some people might look at the morning line to decide whether a horse is an overlay. For example, you might be watching TVG and an announcer says the seven is overbet (an underlay) because its odds are below the morning line. Or the opposite, someone says the horse is an overlay because its odds are above the morning line. Remember that the morning line is only one person's opinion of how the public will bet and not related to the actual chances of any particular horse.

The key to this phrase is determining the actual chances of a particular horse, not comparing a horse's odds to someone else's opinion.

The second half of this hypothesis, "you can't win betting the favorite" is a fallacy for many of the reasons above. The reasoning is based on statistical studies conducted on thousands of races that conclude if you bet the favorite in every race, you will lose money. Most of these studies show a loss of about 10 percent by betting the favorite in every race. But the reason this hypothesis is a myth is that, while betting the favorite in every race would show a long-term loss, any individual favorite may actually be an overlay, or a good bet. In other words, some favorites are overbet in relation to their actual chances, and some favorites are underbet in relation to their actual chances.

The point of all this is: Don't be turned off if the horse you like is the favorite. If you feel that horse's chances justify a wager based on the odds on the tote board, make the bet.

6. "Always back up longshots with a place bet."

You may hear this all the time. It suggests if you like a longshot, such as a 15-1 shot to win, you should also back the horse up with a place bet. The reasoning behind this phrase is that if you are mostly right and your horse runs well without winning, the place and show payoffs will still be good.

There are two general problems with this thinking. The first is that while you know the win payoff (based on the odds), the place payoff may vary, depending on which two horses run first and second. For example, if your 15-1 shot runs second to a heavily bet favorite, your place price will tend to be much lower than if your 15-1 shot finished second to another longshot. If you are betting to place, you are also hoping for another longshot to finish in the top two with your horse.

The other problem is that, in general, the public tends to overbet longshots to place and show and also to underbet favorites to place and show. Many statistical studies have been done on win versus place versus show wagering, and because of human nature and the belief of many players to bet longshots to place and show, those longshots tend to be overbet in the place and show pools. The opposite applies to favorites. People tend to bet favorites to win but ignore the place and show pools fearing a low payoff.

When you first start out at the track, you will probably want to bet horses to place and show, and this is a great way to start. After you become comfortable with playing both straight and exotic wagers, if you like a longshot, in addition to playing the horse to win, you may want to consider exacta boxes rather than a place bet in case your horse runs second. Your return will be much higher.

By John Lindley

Frequently Asked Questions

What do win, place, and show mean?

Win means first, place means second, and show means third. If you bet to win, the horse must finish first for you to be able to cash the ticket. If you bet to place, the horse must be first or second. If you bet to show, the horse must run first, second, or third.

What is the minimum wager?

Bets to win, place, and show must be at least $2, while many wagers such as exactas and trifectas can be made for $1.

How do I know the number of the horse I want to bet on?

Purchase a track program when entering the track. The number next to the horse's name in the track program is the number you use when wagering.

How do I place a wager?

Bets may be made at any window. The proper way to call out a wager, whether straight or exotic, is as follows: amount of the bet, type of bet, and program number of the horse you wish to wager on. For example: $2 to win on number three.

What is the safest wager to make?

If you bet to show and the horse finishes first, second, or third, the ticket may be cashed.

What is a SAM machine?

It is a self-betting machine. The "SAM" stands for Screen Activated Machine. You can purchase a voucher from a mutuel teller or use a winning ticket to place a bet.

What is a daily double?

The daily double is a wager that requires selecting the winners of two consecutive races. Many tracks used to offer the daily double only

Use a horse's program number to bet.

on the first two races each day; now, daily doubles are often offered on any two consecutive races.

What is a longshot?

A horse that will pay a big price if it wins is often called a longshot.

What if I have a winning ticket?

Tickets may also be cashed at any window. There is no hurry to cash a ticket; tickets may be cashed at any time. State laws mandate tickets may be cashed for a specified period of time. In many states, this is one year.

What do I do if I lose a winning mutuel ticket?

Go immediately to a mutuel teller, and the teller may be able to place a "hold" on the ticket and trace the ticket if it hasn't been cashed by someone else.

How often do favorites win?

This varies, but a general rule of thumb is that the favorite in the race — the horse that the most money is bet on to win — will win approximately a third of the time.

I heard someone say they boxed an exacta. What does that mean?

An exacta involves selecting the first two finishers in a race in the "exact" order. If you box two horses, they may finish first or second in either order, and you are able to cash the ticket. If you were going to bet a $2 exacta on numbers five and six, a box would cost $4, but they could finish 5-6 or 6-5.

What is the difference between an exacta and a quinella?

An exacta requires selecting the first two finishers in a race in the exact order. A quinella means the

You can cash a winning ticket anytime after a race is made official.

The 1 and 1A indicate an entry.

is run. The final odds are determined by the bettors' selections.

I saw in the program a horse numbered 1 and another numbered 1A. What does this mean?

This is called an "entry." This means the horses are owned by the same person (wholly or in partnership) or trained by the same person. If you wager on #1 to win, you receive both horses. If either the 1 or 1A wins, you cash your ticket.

horses may finish in either order. Because it is easier to select two horses that may finish in either order, the quinella generally pays less than the exacta.

What is a trifecta?

A trifecta involves choosing the first three finishers in a race in the exact order.

What is a pick three?

This very popular wager involves selecting the winners of three consecutive races. For example, a pick three on races four, five, and six means you must select the winners of all three races to cash the tickets.

What does the phrase "bet down" refer to?

Let's say a horse is 10-1; then you notice his odds are 5-1, and finally when the race starts he is 3-1. Someone may say, "He was really bet down." It means that a sizeable amount of money was wagered on

What do I do if I bet on a horse to win, place, or show and he is scratched before the race?

When a horse is scratched prior to the start of the race, all wagers on that horse are refunded.

Wagering Menu

$2 Win / Place / Show
$2 Exacta
$2 Quinella
$2 Trifecta

A wagering menu is given for each race in the track program.

What is the morning line?

The morning line is one handicapper's opinion of what the odds will be on the horses when the race a horse, causing his odds to go downward.

What does "across the board" mean?

It means betting a horse to win, place, and show. For a $2 wager, this would cost $6 and the ticket would be cashable if the horse runs first, second, or third.

What does "wheel" mean?

A "wheel" bets one horse with all others in a race. A "part-wheel" bets one horse with some others in the race. For instance, if you think #4 is going to win, you can use all other horses in second and bet a exacta wheel: 4 with all. If you think #2, #8, or #9 could run second, you can bet an exacta part-wheel: 4 with 2, 8, and 9.

What do the terms "handle" and "purse" mean?

The "handle" is the amount of money bet or handled that day at the track. The purse means the amount of money the horses can win in a particular race.

Glossary

Across the board — a bet on a horse to win, place, and show. The minimum bet is $6 because three wagers ($2 to win, $2 to place, $2 to show) are being placed. If the horse wins, the bettor receives win, place, and show payouts. If the horse finishes second, the bettor receives place and show payouts, and if the horse finishes third, the bettor receives the show payout.

Allowance race — an event other than claiming for which the racing secretary drafts certain conditions.

Allowances — weights and other conditions of a race.

Also-eligible — a horse officially entered but not permitted to start unless the field is reduced by scratches below a specified number.

Apprentice allowance — weight concession to an apprentice rider. This varies among states from five to ten pounds. Slang term is "bug." Indicated by an asterisk next to the jockey's name in the program.

Baby race — a race for two-year-olds.

Backside — a racetrack's barn or stable area.

Backstretch — the straight part of the track on the far side between turns; slang term to describe the barn or stable area.

Bandage — strips of cloth wound around the lower part of horses' legs for support or protection against injury.

Bar shoe — a horseshoe closed at the back to help support the frog and heel of the hoof. Often worn by horses with quarter cracks or bruised feet.

Bay — a horse's coat color ranging from tan to auburn. The mane and tail are always black as are the lower portion of the legs (black points), except for any white markings.

Beyer speed figure — a handicapping tool, developed by sports writer Andy Beyer of *The Washington Post*, assigning a numerical value to each race run by a horse based on final time and track condition.

Bleeder — a horse that bleeds from the lungs after or during a workout or race.

Blinkers — device to limit a horse's vision to prevent him from swerving from objects, other horses, etc., on either side of him.

Board — the "tote" or totalizator board, which displays odds, betting pools, and other race information.

Bottom line — the lower half of a pedigree diagram, indicating the female side of a horse's bloodlines.

Bounce — a poor performance followed by an exceptionally good one.

Box — a wagering term denoting a bet in which all possible numeric combinations are covered.

Breakage — at pari-mutuel betting tracks, the rounding off to a nickel or dime, as required by state laws, in paying off winning tickets. The breakage is usually split between the track and the state in varying proportions.

Bug boy — an apprentice jockey.

Bullet — fastest workout of the day at a particular distance. A bullet (•) precedes the work time in listings.

Butazolidin (Bute) — the trade name for phenylbutazone, a non-steroidal anti-inflammatory drug.

Chalk — the wagering favorite in a race. The term dates from the days when on-track bookmakers would write odds on a chalkboard.

Chestnut — a horse's coat color ranging from golden to red to chocolate (liver chestnut). Mane and tail are usually the same shade as the body; also, a small, horny growth on the inside of a horse's legs, just above the knee on the forelegs and below the hocks on the hind legs.

Claiming race — an event in which each horse entered is eligible to be purchased at a set price.

Clerk of scales — a racing official whose chief duty is to weigh the riders before and after a race to ensure proper weight is being carried.

Clocker — a person on duty during morning training hours to identify the horses during the workouts, time them, and report to the public their training activities. Some clockers work for the racetrack; others are employed by Equibase.

Clubhouse turn — the first turn past the finish line, where the clubhouse is usually located.

Colors — a horse owner's racing silks, jacket, and cap, worn by jockeys to denote the horse's ownership. All colors are different, and many are registered with The Jockey Club.

Colt — a male Thoroughbred horse (other than a gelding or ridgeling) that has not reached his fifth birth date or has not been bred.

Commingle — combining mutuel pools from off-track sites with the host track.

Condition book — a series of booklets issued by a racing secretary that lists the races to be run at a particular racetrack.

Conformation — the physical appearance or qualities of a horse.

Controlled medication — a term widely used to mean that some drugs, primarily phenylbutazone and furosemide (see Lasix), are permissible under controlled circumstances that allow veterinary administration of predetermined dosages at predetermined intervals prior to race time.

Coupled — two or more horses running as a single betting unit. Also known as an entry.

Daily double — a type of wager calling for the selection of the winners of two consecutive races, usually the first and second on the race card but can be any two consecutive races.

Dam — the female parent of a horse.

Dark bay or brown — a horse's coat color that ranges from brown with areas of tan on the shoulders, head, and flanks, to a dark brown, with tan areas only in the flanks and/or muzzle (nose). The mane, tail, and lower legs are black.

Dead heat — two or more horses finishing on even terms.

Declared — a horse withdrawn from a stakes race in advance of the scratch time on the day of the race.

Derby — a stakes race for three-year-olds.

Distaff — a race for female horses.

Dogs — barriers placed on a track away from the inside rail to indicate that the inside strip of the track is not to be used during morning workouts to preserve the surface. Workouts around these barriers are noted, and the times are correspondingly slower due to the longer distance added on the turns.

Dosage — a form of pedigree analysis, popularized by Dr. Steven Roman, that has become mainly associated with determining whether Kentucky Derby contenders can go a mile and a quarter. The system looks at patterns of ability in horses based on a list of prepotent sires, each of whom is called a *chef-de-race*. Each sire is put in one of five categories: brilliant, intermediate, classic, solid, and professional, which quantify speed and stamina.

Eighth — an eighth of a mile; a furlong; 220 yards; 660 feet.

Entry — two or more horses representing the same owner and/or trainer and running together as a single betting entity. (See Coupled.)

Exacta — to win, a bettor must pick the horses that finish first and second in exact order.

Exacta box — a way to guarantee the outcome of the first two finishers regardless of which horse wins.

Exotic wager — also called a combination wager; a wager that involves two or more horses.

Far turn — the turn or bend in the racetrack opposite the first or clubhouse turn.

Fast (track) — condition of the track surface whereby the footing is dry, even, and resilient.

Field — mutuel field; one or more starters running coupled as a single betting unit. Usually horses determined to have a small chance to win are grouped in the "field." Also used as a term for all the horses in a race.

Filly — a female Thoroughbred that has not reached her fifth birth date or has not been bred.

Firm (track) — condition of turf course surface corresponding to a fast surface on the dirt or main track.

First turn — the bend of track beyond starting point. Also known as the clubhouse turn.

Flat race — a contest on level ground as opposed to a hurdle race, a steeplechase, or a harness race.

Foul — an action by a horse or a jockey that hinders or interferes with another horse or jockey in the running of a race.

Fractional time — intermediate times in a race, as at the quarter-mile, half-mile, three-quarters, etc.

Front-runner — a horse whose usual running style is to get to the lead or near the lead soon after the start of the race and stay there as long as possible.

Full brother (or sister) — horses that have the same sire and dam.

Furlong — one-eighth of a mile; 220 yards; 660 feet.

Furosemide — a diuretic medication often used to treat horses that suffer from exercise induced pulmonary hemorrhage (bleeding) at racetracks. Legal to use under certain conditions in most states. Commonly called by its former brand name, Lasix, although the newer brand name is Salix.

Gelding — a male horse that has been castrated.

Good (track) — condition of track surface between fast and slow as surface dries out.

Graded stakes — a stakes race determined by the American Graded Stakes Committee to receive a grade level of I, II, or III, depending on past field quality, among other factors. American races were first graded in 1973.

Granddam — the grandmother of a horse.

Grandsire — the grandfather of a horse.

Gray — a horse's coat color that is composed of a mixture of black and white hairs. Beginning with foals of 1993, The Jockey Club classifies a gray horse as "gray/roan."

Group race — also known as pattern races; the European equivalent of graded stakes.

Half brother (sister) — horses that have the same dam. Does not apply to horses that share only the same sire.

Hand — four inches; unit used in measuring a horse's height from the ground to the withers.

Handicap — a race in which the racing secretary determines the weight each horse will carry according to his assessment of the horse's ability relative to that of the other horses in the field. The better the horse the more weight he would carry to give each horse a theoretically equal chance of winning.

Handicapper — one who handicaps races, officially or privately; expert who makes selections for publication. Also, name given to the racing secretary who assigns weights for handicaps at his track. Also, a horse that usually runs in handicap races.

Handicapping — the study of all factors in past performances to determine the relative qualities of horses in a race in order to place a bet. These factors include distance, weight, track conditions, trainers, jockeys, breeding, etc.

Handle (mutuel) — the amount of money bet on a race, a daily card, or the total amount bet during the meeting, season, or year at a track.

High weight — highest weight assigned or carried in a race.

Homebred — a horse bred by its owner.

Horse — any Thoroughbred regardless of sex; specifically, an entire male, five years old or older or any male that has been bred.

Inquiry — when track stewards review a race to check for a foul or other infraction of the rules of racing. Also, a sign flashed on the tote board on such occasions to alert bettors to hold their tickets until the race is made official.

In the money — when a horse finishes in first, second, or third.

Intertrack wagering — ITW; wagering on a simulcast race from another track.

Jockey — a professional race rider.

The Jockey Club — the official registry of the American Thoroughbred. Incorporated in 1894 in New York City, The Jockey Club maintains the *American Stud Book*, a register of all Thoroughbreds foaled in the United States, Puerto Rico, and Canada.

Jumper — a steeplechase or hurdle horse.

Juvenile — a two-year-old horse.

Key horse — a single horse used in multiple combinations in an exotic wager.

Lasix — the former brand name for furosemide, a diuretic commonly administered to racehorses. Denoted in programs by an "L"; new brand name is Salix.

Late double — a second daily double offered during the latter part of the race card.

Lay-up — a racehorse sent from the racetrack to a farm or training center to recuperate from injury or illness or to be rested.

Lead — the leading leg of a horse. A horse usually leads with his inside leg around turns and with his opposite leg on straightaways.

Length — a measurement approximating the length of a horse from nose to tail, about eight feet. Distance between horses in a race; calculated as one-fifth of a second in terms of time.

Listed race — an ungraded stakes race.

Maiden — a racehorse of either sex that has never won a race; a female horse that has never been bred. Also, a race classification open only to horses that have never won a race.

Mare — a female Thoroughbred five years old or older, or younger if she has been bred.

Medication list — a list maintained by the track's veterinarian and published by the track showing which horses have been treated with legally prescribed medications.

Minus pool — a mutuel pool caused when a horse is so heavily bet that after deductions of state tax and commission, there is not enough money left to pay the legally prescribed minimum on each winning bet. The racetrack usually makes up the difference.

Morning line — odds quoted in the official program at the track and are the odds at which betting opens.

Mudder — a horse that runs best on a muddy or soft track.

Muddy (track) — condition of track surface that is wet but has no standing water.

Mutuel pool — pari-mutuel pool; sum of the wagers on a race or event, such as the win pool, exacta pool, etc.

Mutuel window — a place at a racetrack or other betting facility where a person goes to make a wager or to collect winnings.

Near side — left side of a horse; a horse is mounted from this side.

Oaks — a stakes event for three-year-old fillies.

Objection — a claim of foul lodged by one jockey against another.

Odds-on — a payoff that would be less than even money.

Off side — right side of a horse.

Off track — a track that is not fast.

Official — a sign displayed when results are confirmed. Or, a racing official.

Off the board — describes a horse that finishes worse than third.

Off-track betting — OTB; wagering at legalized betting outlets run by racetracks, companies specializing in pari-mutuel betting, or, in New York State, by independent companies chartered by the state. Wagers at OTBs are usually commingled with on-track betting pools.

On the board — describes a horse that finishes first, second, or third.

Out of the money — a horse that finishes worse than third.

Overlay — a horse whose odds are greater than its potential to win.

Overnight — a sheet published by the racing secretary's office listing the entries for an upcoming race card.

Overnight race — a race in which entries close a specific number of hours before running (ex: 48 hours), as opposed to a stakes race for which nominations close weeks or months in advance.

Pacesetter — a horse that is running in front or on the lead.

Paddock — area where horses are saddled and paraded before a race.

Pari-mutuel — the form of wagering existing at all U.S. tracks today in which odds are determined by the amount of money bet on each horse. In essence, bettors are competing against each other not against the track, which acts as an agent, taking a commission on each bet to cover purses, taxes, and operating expenses.

Parlay — a multi-race bet in which winnings are subsequently bet on each succeeding race.

Part-wheel — using a key horse(s) in different, but not all possible, exotic wagering combinations.

Past performances — a line-by-line listing of a horse's race record, plus earnings, connections, bloodlines, and other pertinent information.

Patrol judges — officials who observe the progress of a race from various vantage points around the racing strip.

Pedigree — a written record of a Thoroughbred's family tree.

Phenylbutazone — a non-steroidal anti-inflammatory medication legal in certain amounts for racehorses in many states. Normally administered 24 to 48 hours before race time. Also called Bute or Butazolidin.

Photo finish — a result so close that the stewards have to review the finish-line photo to determine the order of finish.

Pick (number) — a type of multi-race wager in which the winners of designated races must be picked. Ex: pick three, pick six.

Placed — finishing second or third in a race. A stakes-placed horse is one that has finished second or third in a stakes but has not won a stakes.

Place bet — a wager in which the bettor collects if the horse finishes first or second. However, if the horse wins, the bettor receives only the place payout.

Plater — a horse that runs in claiming races.

Points of call — a horse's position at various locations on the racetrack where its running position is noted on a chart. The locations vary with the race distance and usually correspond to the fractional times also noted on the chart.

Pole — markers placed at measured distances around the track and identified by distance from the finish line. Ex: The quarter pole is a quarter of a mile from the finish.

Pool — the total money bet on entire field to win, place, and show.

Post parade — horses going from the paddock to the starting gate (post), parading past the stands.

Post position — a position in the starting gate from which a horse breaks. Numbered from the rail outward.

Post time — the designated time for a race to start.

Prep — training; an event that precedes another, more important, engagement.

Purse — a race for money or other prize to which the owners do not contribute.

Quinella — a wager in which the first two finishers must be picked in either order.

Rabbit — a speed horse running as an entry with another, usually late-running horse. The rabbit is expected to set a fast pace to help its stablemate's chances.

Race-day medication — medication given on race day; most medications, with the exception of Lasix, are prohibited in almost all racing jurisdictions.

Racing secretary — an official who drafts conditions for races, writes the condition book, and usually serves as handicapper.

Restricted race — a race restricted to certain starters either because of their place of birth or their previous winnings.

Roan — a horse's coat color that is a mixture of red and white hairs or brown and white hairs. The Jockey Club classifies this coat color under the label "gray/roan."

Route — broadly, a race distance of longer than a mile and an eighth.

Run down — when the pasterns of a horse hit the track in a race or workout, causing abrasions. Also a bandage to prevent injury from running down.

Saddle cloth — a cloth under the saddle on which the number denoting the horse's post position is displayed for races.

Scale of weights — fixed imposts to be carried by horses in a race, determined according to age, sex, season, and distance.

Scratch — to remove a horse from a race before the race goes off.

Show — third position at the finish.

Show bet — a wager in which the bettor collects if his horse finishes first, second, or third, but he only collects the show payout.

Silks — the jacket and cap worn by riders.

Simulcast — a live television transmission of a race to other tracks, off-track betting facilities, or other outlets for wagering.

Sire — the father of a horse; a stallion that has produced a foal that has won a race.

Sixteenth — one-sixteenth of a mile; a half-furlong; 110 yards; 330 feet.

Sloppy (track) — condition of track surface in which it is saturated with water and standing water is visible.

Slow (track) — condition of track surface in which the surface and base are both wet.

Soft (track) — condition of the turf course with a large amount of moisture.

Sophomore — a three-year-old horse.

Sound — term used to denote a Thoroughbred's health and freedom from disease or lameness.

Speed figure — a handicapping tool used to assign a numerical value to a horse's performance. See Beyer speed figure.

Sprint — a race distance of less than one mile in Thoroughbred racing.

Stakes — the highest class of race. A race in which an entry fee is paid by the owners of the horses starting and those entry fees are added to the purse; thus, a stakes is often referred to as an added-money race. Also, invitational races (no entry fee required) with a large purse (usually $50,000 or more) are regarded as stakes races.

Stakes-placed — when a horse finishes second or third in a stakes.

Stakes horse — a horse that competes mainly in stakes race but that may not have actually won a stakes.

Stallion — an entire male horse used for the purpose of breeding.

Starter — a racing official in charge of the starting gate. A horse that runs in a race.

Starter allowance — a particular kind of race written to allow claiming horses that have improved from their earlier form to run in a non-claiming event.

Starter handicap — the same type of race as a starter allowance except that the horses are assigned weights by the handicapper rather than determining them from allowance conditions.

State-bred — a horse bred and/or foaled in a particular state in a manner that meets all the criteria set down by state law and racing commission rules, and thus is eligible to compete in special races.

Stayer — a horse that can run long distances.

Stewards — racing officials who uphold the rules of racing at a racetrack. They answer to the state racing commission, and their decisions can be appealed to that body.

Steeplechase — a race in which horses jump over a series of obstacles on a turf course.

Straight wager — a wager to win, place, or show.

Stretch — the homestretch; straightaway portion of a racetrack in front of the grandstand.

Stretch runner — a horse that runs its fastest nearing the finish of a race.

Superfecta — a wager in which the bettor must pick the first four finishers in a race in exact order.

Takeout (take) — commission deducted from mutuel pools that is shared by the track, horsemen, and the state.

Thoroughbred — a distinctive breed of horse used for flat and steeplechase racing.

Tongue-tie — a strap or tape bandage used to tie down a horse's tongue to prevent it from choking him in a race or workout.

Top line — a Thoroughbred's breeding on the sire's side (sire line). Also, the visual line created by the horse's back.

Top weight — the high weight in a race.

Totalizator — an intricate machine that sells betting tickets, records total of straight win, place, and show pools, and keeps track of amount bet on each horse in the three categories; shows odds to win on each horse in the field and complete payoffs after the finish.

Tote board — the electronic totalizator display in the infield, which presents up-to-the-minute odds. It also may show the amounts wagered in each mutuel pool as well as information on jockey and equipment changes, etc.

Track bias — a racing surface that seems to favor a particular running style, such as front-running, or position, such as the rail.

Track record — fastest time at various distances made at a particular course.

Trifecta — a wager in which the bettor must pick the first three finishers in a race in exact order.

Trifecta box — a trifecta wager in which all possible combinations using a given number of horses are bet upon.

Turf — grass as opposed to dirt racing surfaces; when capitalized in a sentence, denotes the entire racing industry.

Turn downs — rear shoes that are turned down three-quarters of an inch to an inch at the ends to provide better traction on an off track. This kind of shoe is illegal in some racing jurisdictions.

Underlay — a horse bet at shorter odds than would appear warranted judging by its past performances.

Walkover — a race in which only one horse competes after all others are scratched or no other horses are entered.

Washy — when a horse breaks out in a nervous sweat before a race.

Weight-for-age — fixed scale of weights to be carried by horses according to age, sex, distance of race, and month.

Wheel — betting all possible combinations in an exotic wager using at least one horse as the key.

Wire-to-wire — to lead in a race from the gate to the finish line.

Work — to exercise a horse; a workout.

Yielding — condition of the turf course with a lot of moisture in it causing horses to sink into it noticeably.

Resource Guide

The Blood-Horse
www.bloodhorse.com

Daily Racing Form
www.drf.com

Bloodstock Research Information
   Services
www.brisnet.com

Thoroughbred Daily News
www.thoroughbreddailynews.com

Thoroughbred Sports Network
www.tsnhorse.com

Youbet.com
www.youbet.com

Television Games Network
www.tvg.com

Equine Line
www.equineline.com

Equibase
www.equibase.com

Thoroughbred Pedigree Query
www.pedigreequery.com

Dosage: Pedigree and Performance
www.chef-de-race.com

The Jockey Club Information
   Services
www.tjcis.com

National Thoroughbred Racing
   Association
www.ntra.com

Arlington Park
www.arlingtonpark.com

Calder Racecourse
www.calderracecourse.com

Churchill Downs
www.churchilldowns.com

Delaware Park
www.delawarepark.com

Del Mar
www.dmtc.com

Emerald Downs
www.emdowns.com

Fair Grounds
www.fairgroundsracecourse.com

Gulfstream Park
www.gulfstreampark.com

Hollywood Park
www.hollywoodpark.com

Keeneland
www.keeneland.com

Laurel Park
www.laurelpark.com

Lone Star Park
www.lonestarpark.com

Louisiana Downs
www.ladowns.com

Meadowlands
www.thebigm.com

Monmouth Park
www.monmouthpark.com

New York Racing Association
(Aqueduct, Belmont Park,
Saratoga)
www.nyra.com

Pimlico
www.pimlico.com

Santa Anita
www.santaanita.com

Books

Beyer, Andrew. *Beyer on Speed.*
Boston: Houghton Mifflin Co.,
1993.

Beyer, Andrew. *Picking Winners: A
Horseplayer's Guide.* Boston:
Houghton Mifflin Co., 1994.

Davidowitz, Steve. *Betting
Thoroughbreds: A Professional's
Guide for the Horseplayer.* New
York: Plume Books, 1997.

Free, Brad. *Handicapping 101:
Finding the Right Horses and
Making the Right Bets.* New York:
DRF Press, 2004.

Helm, Mike. *Exploring Pedigree:
Handicapping's Newest Frontier.*
Fort Bragg, CA: City Miner
Books, 1994.

Lindley, John. *Handicapping for
Bettor or Worse.* Lexington, KY.:
Eclipse Press, 2004.

Roman, Steven A. *Dosage: Pedigree
and Performance.* Neenah, WI:
Russell Meerdink Co., 2003.

Stich, Lauren. *Pedigree
Handicapping.* New York: DRF
Press, 2004.

Contributors

Rena Baer is assistant editor for Eclipse Press, the book division of Blood-Horse Publications. She lives in Lexington, Kentucky.

Tom Hall is senior editor for Eclipse Press and co-author of *The Calumet Collection*. He lives in Lexington, Kentucky.

Evan Hammonds is managing editor of *The Blood-Horse* and a former editor at *Daily Racing Form*. He resides in Versailles, Kentucky.

Tom LaMarra is news editor of *The Blood-Horse* and avid handicapper. He lives in Lexington, Kentucky.

Dan Liebman is executive editor of *The Blood-Horse* and has given handicapping seminars to novice bettors at Keeneland. He resides in Frankfort, Kentucky.

John Lindley is author of *Handicapping for Bettor or Worse*, has taught classes on handicapping, and has owned racehorses in partnership. He lives near Seattle, Washington.